RECLAIMING
THE
SOUL

RECLAIMING
THE
SOUL

The Search for
Meaning in a
Self-Centered
Culture

Jeffrey H. Boyd, M.D.

The Pilgrim Press
Cleveland, Ohio

The Pilgrim Press, Cleveland, Ohio 44115
© 1996 by Jeffrey H. Boyd

Biblical quotations are from the New Revised Standard Version of the Bible, © 1989 by the Division of Christian Education of the National Council of the Churches of Christ in the U.S.A., and are used by permission

Printed in the United States of America on acid-free paper

01 00 99 98 97 96   5 4 3 2 1

Library of Congress Cataloging-in-Publication Data

Boyd, Jeffrey H.
   Reclaiming the soul : the search for meaning in a self-centered culture / Jeffrey H. Boyd.
      p.   cm.
   Includes bibliographical references and index.
   ISBN 0-8298-1080-3 (alk. paper)
   1. Soul.   2. Psychiatry and religion.   3. Christianity—Psychology.
I. Title
BT741.2.B683   1996
233'.5—dc20   95-51177
                                                         CIP

To Maureen C. O'Brien and
Gordon R. Lewis

CONTENTS

ACKNOWLEDGMENTS

I AM INDEBTED TO many people who made this book possible. First there is the patient tolerance of my family: Maureen O'Brien, Matthew, Felicity, and Ruth Boyd. Brilliant scholars in the theological realm have taught me most of what I know: Doctor Gordon R. Lewis, Professor James Barr, Krister Stendahl, Professor Brevard S. Childs, Professor John W. Cooper, Professor Bruce A. Demarest, Father David Q. Liptak, Augustine, Tertullian, Gregory of Nyssa, Justin Martyr, Thomas Aquinas, Martin Luther, John Calvin, John Wesley, Franz Delitzsch, Johannes Pedersen, Karl Barth, Reinhold Niebuhr, Oscar Cullmann, and Oskar Pfister. I want to thank Presiding Bishop Edmond L. Browning of the Episcopal church for his encouragement. Dr. Leonard Sweet, publisher of *Sweet's Soul Cafe,* provided inspiration.

The staff of Pilgrim Press have been unbelievably helpful in encouraging me and helping me organize this material, especially Richard Brown, Kelley Baker, Marjorie Pon, Martha Clark, Madrid Tramble, Ed Huddleston, Carole Downes, Paul Tuttle, and freelance copyeditor Craig Kirkpatrick. I have received endless reservoirs of encouragement from Dr. Kenneth L. Barker, Dr. David B. Larson, Dr. Freeman Barton, Dr. Steven Schneider, Bill Fay, Catherine Kroeger, Sarah Smith, Rick and Rosemary Matson, Sue and Dave Gearhart, Rev. Peter and Kathy Rodgers, Richard and Pat O'Brien, Dr. Darrel A. Regier, Dr. David Sabine, Dr. Ernst Prelinger, Dr. Alan Broadhead, Dr. John Mason, and Dr. John Young.

Waterbury Hospital's library staff have given tremendous help, especially Nancy Testa, Robin Ackley, and Carol Youle. I am indebted to the staff of Waterbury Hospital Health Center for their supportive efforts, most especially Margaret Benner, Carol "Hogan" Gallucci, Dr. Scott Somerville, Rose Ciardiello, Ellen Ebbs, Doreen Elnitsky, Lucille Janatka, John Tobin, Frank Fabiano, Esther Montalvo, Donna Hanson, Patricia Robinson, Barbara Ann Civitello, Patricia Sullivan, Barbara Miller, Anne Adamski, Ann Griffin, Pat Pellegrino, Carrie Minor, Rosemary Kenney, Sabina Loyot, Doris Fox, Carol Gasper, Philomena Perugini, Andrea Mayshaw, Annette Derouin, Terri Cimino, Terri Franz, John Smith, Sandy Mattson, Gail Yoder, Rita Moisao, Sandra Santarsiero, Grace Labriola, Susan Czarkosky, Anne Lund, Jeanne McGuire, Cindy Coleman, Sharon Croteau, Don Gaeta, Barbara Benevento, Barbara McGeever, Mildred Perreault, Linda Snitkin, Jean Horan, Barbara Keane, Ann Soule, Mindy Daskal, Elaine Poulos, Jeannette Rossi, Chris Fillie, Lou Daly, Irene Fazio, Mary Ann Bielik, Susan Kilby, Paul Lapotosky, Domenic Biello, Mark Sconziano, Jackie Sullivan, Bruce Baker, Michael Higgison, David Howe, Carol Cestaro, Jennifer DiTunno, Sandra Fitzgerald, Jodi Kalat, James McMinn, Anthony Leonardi, James Orgel, Michele Gillette, Laurie Gambardella, Anthony Bocci, Michael Lawlor, Dr. Lori Sobel, Dr. Alex Demac, Tracy Violette, Maureen Curtis, Kim Perugini, Lisa Biello, Edwin Cole, Marci Berlin, John Veronesi, Nancy Kowalczyk, Elaine Phillips, Patrick Raymond, Joanne Seymour, Marie Russo, Roni Sheehy, Nancy Stevens, Maryann Zurolo, Larry Moskowitz, Dr. Kinson Lee, Dr. Sreedevi Nampoothiri, Dr. Charles Atkins, Dr. Marshall Wold, Dr. Leonard Stern, Dr. Julia Knerr, Billy Nelson, Dennise Murray Boyle, Julie Mave, Carol Stopper, Amy Sochocki-Norton, Tracy Tuthill, Dr. Emily Littman, and Vinnie Dobas.

My deceased wife, Patricia T. Boyd, and my deceased son, Justin, taught me the meaning of death. My deceased father, Francis O. Boyd, showed me what it would be like to have a mind that could soar like a falcon. Those who converted me to Christianity deserve special thanks: Fra Angelica, who painted *Jesus and the Magdalene* on the wall of the Monastery of San Marco in Florence, and George Frideric Handel, who wrote the *Messiah*.

INTRODUCTION

I AM AN EXPERT ON the psychiatric and Christian views of the soul. Call me a psychiatric Dr. Jekyll and an ordained Reverend Hyde.

A quarter of a century ago I was praying that God use me for whatever purpose God wanted. At that time I was ordained, but I had never even thought of going to medical school. During those prayers I repeatedly felt called to write a book on the soul. I told God I would not do so for two reasons. First, I knew that the soul had been discredited in theology; my New Testament teacher at Harvard Divinity School, Krister Stendahl, had been one of the leaders in the antisoul movement in theology.[1] Second, I felt that psychiatrists were treating the soul, and at that time I had not been to medical school and had no training in mental health.

Today, I am a physician who has been on the psychiatry faculty of the National Institutes of Health and Yale Medical School; published psychiatric articles in the *New England Journal of Medicine*, the *American Journal of Psychiatry*, and the *Archives of General Psychiatry*; written chapters in leading psychiatric textbooks; and helped to write the diagnostic system used today in the mental health field. I am also a theologian who has preached, led worship services, published in leading theological journals, and spoken about the soul before the American Academy of Religion and the Evangelical Theological Society. I have taught about the soul at evangelical and liberal seminaries, at secular hospitals, and at Yale Medical School and Yale Di-

vinity School.[2] I am a member of the Society of Biblical Literature, and my work on the soul has been reported in the *New
York Times*.[3]

I write all this not to overwhelm the reader with my creden-
tials, but to suggest that I know something about neuro-
transmitters and spirits. I am familiar with Freud, biological
psychiatry, and the Bible. Those experiencing a dark night of the
soul have come to me for help, both as a psychotherapist and as
a pastor. Schizophrenics have told me they feel dignity because
they are children of God. Christians have told me that they hide
their faith from other therapists because, as it is written in
Matthew 7:6, they don't want to cast their pearls before pigs.

But I am lonely. My fellow psychiatrists don't want to talk
with me about the soul. And when I approach biblical scholars
about the subject, they usually tell me to avoid the very word
because it has Platonic connotations and has been long banished
from Christian religion (as I discuss in chapter 2). I feel like a
duckbilled platypus. Just as a platypus is neither mammal nor
bird, so I am viewed as an odd but interesting anomaly by
colleagues in both psychiatry and the ministry. Therefore I feel
intellectually isolated—except for the vast number of lay people, many of whom are my patients, who are hungry for information about the soul.

Throughout my career I have tried to merge the two sides of
my brain, to overcome this division in my professional personality. That rift or canyon that runs down the center of American
culture, dividing the world of psychotherapy from the world of
Christianity, is an internal split in my own identity, which I have
overcome by studying what the Bible really says about the soul.
In the process, I have come to conclude that psychiatrists are
leading Americans in the wrong direction.

I believe that secular psychotherapists routinely treat the
soul—without knowing it. Evidence that psychotherapists
treat the soul will be forthcoming, later in this book. Needless
to say, such a belief is not widely shared by my colleagues in the
profession. (Interestingly, the Greek word for soul is *psyche*, as

in the word "psychiatry."[4] As Freud wrote, "Treatment of the psyche means . . . treatment of the soul. One could also understand it to mean treatment of sickness when it occurs in the life of the soul."[5]) The soul has been misunderstood. Although many Americans, even many clergy, look to mental health experts for advice about human nature, human nature cannot be understood from a secular point of view. To understand the soul, we must begin with God and our relationship with God. Clergy, ultimately, are far more important in the treatment of the soul than are psychotherapists.[6]

Therapists usually avoid any mention of God. Only 43 percent of psychiatrists and psychologists claim they believe in God[7]— less than half of the 94 percent of the American people who claim to be believers.[8] Some psychologists, such as Albert Ellis, are openly hostile, contending that religion equals "irrational thinking and emotional disturbance."[9]

Although there is a covert hostility to religion among many therapists, psychotherapy still is often helpful to Christians if their faith is acknowledged and treated with respect. This has even been demonstrated in a controlled clinical trial by Dr. Rebecca Propst, in which depressed Christians were randomly assigned to different forms of therapy, some of which acknowledged and others of which did not acknowledge the patient's faith.[10] Only when the client's faith was acknowledged was the psychotherapy effective.

I have been to several psychotherapists. The one who helped the most, by far, was ironically a Freudian, Dr. Ernst Prelinger. Why was he so helpful? Because he acknowledged the central psychological problem of my life: God. Early in treatment he said, "It may be that you are in so much pain because you feel called by God. It could be that you have a religious, not a neurotic, problem."

Prelinger taught me that the goal of psychotherapy is to allow us to decrease the extent to which we live on the basis of lies, denial, and rationalizations. It allows us to face the truth. Lies and denial don't come from God (John 8:44). In this respect, many Christians have found that therapy helps them pursue the goals of regeneration and sanctification. Therapy is really dangerous only if it treats one's faith with contempt or with silent disdain.

How do you find a trustworthy therapist? Ask your minister.

In this book I will show that the word "soul" has been lost from our vocabulary. My reason for wanting to recover the term is that I believe that Christianity and the Bible have a psychological message, a message that cannot simply be ignored. I stand in the long tradition that considers the Bible to be the greatest textbook of psychology ever written.

Let us assume, for a moment, that psychotherapists treat the soul. Do they do an adequate job? Are their assumptions about the nature of the soul correct? How does the psychotherapy soul compare with the biblical soul?

Christ's central teaching about life is that it is paradoxical: One who seeks life (or *psyche*) will lose it; one who loses it for Christ will find it (Matt. 16:25; Mark 8:35; Luke 9:24, 17:33; John 12:25).

Why is psychotherapy headed in the wrong direction? If secular therapists teach clients to seek themselves, to try to discover the vitality of their hearts, then they are traveling down a dead-end road of frustration. The self-centered goal of maximizing potential, fulfilling aspirations, and seeking autonomy, self-determination, and individuation is the road to destruction, according to Christ (Matt. 7:13–14; Mark 8:34–38; Luke 9:23–26). Christianity is not about seeking to fulfill yourself, but about God seeking us. Self-denial and self-sacrifice are central in my understanding of the New Testament. Those who lose their lives (or lose themselves) for Christ will be given the vitality of life as a gift from God. Lose yourself for Christ and, paradoxically, you will discover who you really are.

I define the term "soul" in this way: *the inner or subjective person in the natural state, whether saved or unsaved.* Everyone is a soul. But "soul" is a rich and evocative term with many other overtones and connotations (which I explore in chapter 5).

This primary definition of the soul needs to be nuanced and elaborated. From an ontological point of view, we are composed of only two parts, what the New Testament calls the "inside" and the "outside" (Matt. 7:15, 23:25–28; Mark 7:15, 18, 21–23; Luke 11:39; Rom. 7:22; 2 Cor. 4:16, 7:5; Eph. 3:16–17; 1 Pet. 3:3–4). The "outside" terminates at death and resumes at resurrection. The "inside" persists and can be called either "soul," "spirit," or "heart." Thus from an ontological viewpoint, soul and spirit are identical. (Ontology is the branch of philosophy that concerns how many fundamentally different sorts of entities exist.)

From a functional viewpoint, however, there is both overlap between the words soul and spirit, and a difference in emphasis. In the Bible the word "soul" emphasizes the horizontal aspect of the inner person, relating person to person and person to environment. The word "spirit" emphasizes the vertical aspect of the inner person, relating human to God and vice versa. But there is only one, indivisible inner person. This issue will be discussed further in chapter 5.

We need to clarify also what is meant by the phrase "in the natural state." This refers to humans as we observe ourselves today, which is fallen human nature. The word "natural" has two meanings: that which is intrinsic in God's creation, and that which appears to be intrinsic based on what we observe in the fallen world in which we dwell. That which is "natural" to humans as created by God is not completely visible on this earth, for the true human is evident only in three places: Adam and Eve before the fall, Christ, and humans in heaven. I believe that when we get to heaven we will discover that some of what we thought was "natural" inside us will be regenerated away, so that we will discover ourselves to be more fully human, without the junk. In the primary definition of the soul ("inner person in the natural state"), I am using the word to refer to the fallen human nature we observe in ourselves and around us.[11]

As I discuss throughout this book, the word "soul" has been

largely rejected by theologians—especially by biblical scholars, Protestant theologians, and Jewish scholars. (Catholic theologians, as I will demonstrate, are not so antagonistic to the soul.) When theologians seek to develop a soulless religion, they often claim that the word "spirit" is an adequate substitute for the missing word "soul." I disagree. This assumption that we don't need the word "soul" leaves Christians without an adequate vocabulary for dealing with the secular mental health movement. This is a serious problem.

The number of psychotherapists, and likely their influence, in America is doubling every ten years or so. A glance at the *Yellow Pages* reveals that there are more secular psychotherapists than churches and synagogues of all denominations combined.[12] An increasing number of liberal churches are becoming bankrupt; an increasing number of psychotherapists are becoming rich. Almost 2 percent of the American gross national product is devoted to mental health and substance abuse treatment.[13] Secular mental health is about a $100 billion industry annually in the United States.[14] Popular magazines and television programs promote a secular mental health view of the human soul, a view that assumes human nature can be fully understood without ever mentioning God.

For this reason I think it is essential to discuss the soul. I reject the common assumption among Americans that psychotherapists are the primary experts on everything important about human life—one's emotions, ideas, and intimate relationships—whereas clergy are experts only in the area of abstract theological beliefs.[15]

The following case, drawn from my psychiatric practice, illustrates the difference between mental health and the Christian view of the soul.

Steve is a forty-five-year-old single man who has lived with his parents his whole life. His friends told him that it was time for him to grow up and leave home, that a forty-five-year-old man could not live with abusive parents and be psychologically healthy. Steve was unable to consider leaving home. Instead he felt neurotic, accepted his family's definition of him as "weak," and underwent years of psychotherapy to try to "fix" what was wrong with him. His mother was a paranoid schizophrenic who was often tense about whether the food was poisoned or whether there would soon be an invasion from Jupiter. Steve's father was an angry man, always critical, never pleased. The father had regularly beaten Steve when Steve was an infant. Both parents expressed deep-felt contempt for Steve and for each other.

Over the years Steve had adopted ways of dealing with his parents by hiding his true feelings, sometimes even from himself. Although the parents thought Steve was "weak," he was actually the glue that held the family together, and his affection was essential for the parents' survival. His friends counseled Steve that he should be furious with his parents, but he was unable to feel anger at them. He felt pity, not hatred. His friends told him he needed to make something out of his life, not watch it go down the toilet.

After spending years in psychotherapy with other doctors, Steve came to me for help. After so much exposure to psychotherapists, Steve hoped to get a Ph.D. in psychology and become a therapist himself. He flagellated himself for being too "weak" to be able to leave home and pursue such a career. I listened to him complain about how meek and timid he was, and how neurotic he felt. His friends agreed with these indictments against him.

One day it dawned on me what to say. I told him that he should consider his priorities. He had made it clear to me that his first priority in life was to take care of his crazy parents, who could not survive without him. This was such a high priority for him that he was willing to make any sacrifice to accomplish it. All other priorities would have to play second fiddle. He should stop torturing himself about wanting to get a Ph.D. in psychology, I said, because that was not something he would be able to do without leaving home.

Steve replied that when he got to heaven he knew for sure that Jesus would meet him at the gate and say, "Well done, good and trusted servant, you have served me by taking care of these incapable parents who were assigned to you." It was at that point that I finally realized what Steve's life was all about. His remark astonished him as much as it astonished me.

From that day, Steve's spirit lifted. What had been a humiliating albatross—namely, his inability to leave home—became a source of pride. He felt he was doing God's work. His self-sacrifice and martyrdom were seen as positive rather than neurotic. His unappreciative parents could not actually survive without Steve. Were he to leave home, his parents would probably split up, and his mother would probably become a homeless schizophrenic. He really did feel a religious calling.

I told Steve that I admired him, and that I would gladly trade places with him any day. Although I struggle to serve God, I do not live with a conviction that Jesus will welcome me at the Pearly Gates as a good and trusted servant. I would trade all my accomplishments in life to have what he has: an unshakable conviction that he is doing what he is called to do.

When I lectured about this at an Episcopal church, a woman in the congregation was horrified that I had encouraged what she called "enabling behavior" on Steve's part. She thought I was incompetent as a psychiatrist. It was "unhealthy," she said, for Steve to stay at home and support his crazy parents.

I replied that Steve's life had blossomed ever since he realized that this was his calling as a Christian. He had more self-esteem, enjoyed more hobbies and outside interests, was more able to talk with friends, and no longer felt himself to be weird. Thus, by any method of measuring outcome, his life had improved because I approved of his religious calling.

Steve's transformation represents a Copernican revolution. He finally realized that his whole life made sense only if he assumed that God was the center of value. His self-esteem was not based on being autonomous and independent of God, as his friends and psychotherapists had urged. There was no need for him to "grow up." Steve still lives at home. He no longer feels neurotic. He has discarded the idea of getting a Ph.D. in psychology. He has also come to believe that one of his biggest problems in life has been the mental health movement. Not only have secular psychologists failed to realize what lay at his heart—namely, his faith—but his friends have also been infected by psychological ways of thinking about what is "healthy" and what is "unhealthy." Even clergy who are his friends have regarded him as neurotic. They, too, have assumed that psychological growth and taking good care of oneself are more important than seeking a religiously inspired calling.

This case suggests a critical point I want to make in this book: that self-denial is central to Christian psychology, whereas self-fulfillment is central to the assumptions of secular psychotherapists. Furthermore, the criticism leveled against me by the Christian layperson, indicting me for "enabling" Steve to "enable" his parents, is a vivid illustration of how the Christian church has sold its soul to the devil. I find it remarkable when Christian compassion toward ailing parents is condemned by a Christian as "enabling." Until recently the Fifth Commandment, "Honor your father and your mother," was widely cherished in the Christian church. Today many Christians, inspired by the mental health movement, are endorsing a very different kind of commandment: "Do not honor your father, nor your mother, if it limits self-fulfillment." At this rate, I expect to hear a sermon that mercy and forgiveness are "unhealthy" and constitute "enabling behavior."

I am astonished when clergy, lacking any theory of the soul from the theological world, turn to the secular mental health movement to provide guidance on what is "healthy" and "unhealthy" about people's souls.

My teaching is that a healthy soul is God-centered (see Table 1). There are two advantages to losing oneself, theologically speaking, while devoting oneself to service of God and neighbor:

1. Self-denial in devotion to God leads paradoxically to the richness of this life, because life comes as a gift from God, and is not intrinsic to us.

2. Devotion to God rather than self is the road to salvation on the Day of Judgment.

Most books in which psychotherapists seek to reconcile Christianity and the psychotherapy view of human nature seek to convey this message: feel good about yourself. I disagree. I am convinced that the American people have been bamboozled by psychiatrists, psychologists, social workers, and marriage and family therapists. There is simply too much emphasis on the self, on feeling good about oneself.

We need only consider the following parable told by Jesus if we believe it is essential to feel good about ourselves:

> Who among you would say to your slave who has just come in from plowing or tending sheep in the field, "Come here at once and take your place at the table"? Would you not rather say to him, "Prepare supper for me, put on your apron and serve me while I eat and drink; later you may eat and drink"? Do you thank the slave for doing what was commanded? So you also, when you have done all that you were ordered to do, say, "We are worthless slaves; we have done only what we ought to have done!" (Luke 17:7–10)

Jesus advises the servant to feel unworthy, rather than feeling good about having done an excellent job. Christ urged a lifestyle that no sane American would want if he or she were interested in mere self-esteem.

In my textbook of psychiatry, the Bible, I read that people have a tendency toward narcissism—what theologians call hubris. It is the tendency to believe erroneously that we have the wellspring of life inside ourselves, and the corresponding failure to recognize our dependency on God as the author of our life. Most psychotherapists are teaching people the wrong message, a message that amounts to what Christians have traditionally called "sin."[16] The word "sin" simply means living

TABLE 1 "SOUL" AND "SELF" COMPARED

CHARACTERISTIC	SOUL	SELF
Definition	Inner person in the natural state	Inner person in the natural state
Synonyms	Person, mind, personality, I, identity, subjectivity	Person, mind, personality, I, identity, subjectivity
The center of the universe is	God	Yourself
You are accountable to	God	Yourself
Does God exist?	Yes, God exists.	Who cares?
The greatest source of psychological insight is	The Bible	Your therapist
The ultimate goal of life is	Loving God, serving neighbor	Enjoyment, pleasure, fulfilling your potential, being all that you can be
Is religion part of who you are?	Yes, religion is central to your soul.	Religion is remote, of no psychological importance, peripheral, marginal.
Values are	Essential to the soul	Not part of the self
Life after death is	Important	Irrelevant
Self-sacrifice and self-denial	Essential if you are followers of Christ. They remind us that we are not God.	Questionable activities since they diminish the self.

as if God were not important, which in turn leads to alienation from God.

I have been immersed in the mental health movement most of my adult life. I have hired, taught, supervised, and fired psychiatrists. Therapists of every variety have come to me for teaching, supervision, or therapy. I have treated many thousands of patients. I am an expert witness.

During all this time I have frequently been asked, "How do you feel about that?" Yet never once have I heard a therapist, other than myself, ask, "How does God feel about that? Have you been on your knees recently to ask God about it?" Psychotherapists routinely assume that one's feelings can be trusted. Beneath that assumption is the belief that everyone is fundamentally good (except, of course, those with antisocial personality disorder).

Yet I will make a bold claim: Those who have not turned to God and God alone as their hope are not necessarily good. They tend to have, as the Bible suggests, hard hearts and stiff necks.

On the other hand, those who have given their lives to God are fundamentally different. They have a conflict inside themselves between a self-centered nature (what Paul would call the old Adam) and a God-centered nature (what the New Testament calls the Spirit, or Christ dwelling within). Such people, ironically, are at war with themselves. Paul experienced this: "I do not understand my own actions. For I do not do what I want, but I do the very thing I hate" (Rom. 7:15). In the midst of this struggle, such individuals reveal genuine love of God and neighbor.

I said above that the American people have been bamboozled by secular psychotherapists. But the secular mental health movement is not the only culprit leading us down this path. There are many other reasons for the secularization of America.[17]

Magazines sold at the checkout counters of grocery stores and drugstores promote a new gospel of self-esteem.[18] Replacing Christ's First and Great Commandment is this: you should love your self with all your heart, mind, and strength. The second teaching is like it: you should love your partner as yourself, but only after you have taken good care of yourself. Magazines such as *Self, Redbook, Cosmopolitan,* and *McCall's,* and dozens of secular television shows, suggest that the goal of life is to look inside yourself to find the resources of self-esteem, and to improve your lifestyle. That which popular American culture calls the "self" would traditionally have been called the "soul."[19] But the soul belongs to God. As Saint Augustine said when he looked into his heart, our hearts are restless till they rest in God.[20] And Sigmund Freud wrote: "Only religion can answer the question of the purpose of life. One can hardly go wrong in concluding that the idea of life having a purpose stands or falls with the religious system."[21]

There is hope. The American reading public seems to be fascinated with the soul. Thomas Moore's books on the soul have remained on the *New York Times* best-seller list for years.[22] Moore writes,

> The great malady of the twentieth century, implicated in all our troubles and affecting us individually and socially, is "loss of soul." When soul is neglected, it doesn't just go away; it appears symptomatically in obsessions, addictions, violence, and loss of meaning. Our temptation is to isolate these symptoms or to try to eradicate them one by one; but the root problem is that we have lost our wisdom about the soul, even our interest in it.[23]

That is the most succinct statement of the problem that I have found anywhere. Moore's teaching on the soul is derived from Dr. James Hillman's archetypal psychology, which is in the tradition of Carl Jung.[24] That tradition is different from the perspective of this book.[25] But the important point is that Thomas Moore has awakened all of us to the vast public hunger for information about the soul, and inspired an entirely new market for publishing.[26]

When I talk with theologians about reclaiming the soul because of the threat of the secular mental health movement, they usually shrug their shoulders and respond that the term "spirit" is a sufficient replacement. These conversations leave me frustrated. The absence of the soul is felt to be no problem whatsoever in the eyes of most theologians. In their complacency, they look at me as if my anguish were neurotic, and ask me why I am making such a big issue of an unnecessary word—implying that

I might be better off in a mental hospital than in my office treating clients.

This experience has challenged me, and I have frequently felt pangs of self-doubt. But I persist. My calling to write about the soul, after all, is my "Mission: Impossible." Remember Jonah, who ran away from his calling, was swallowed by a huge fish, and wound up in his destination of Nineveh anyway? I'd rather not take that chance. It is safe to say that I am driven by either obsession or the Spirit of God.

My pilgrimage to reclaim the soul is also motivated by my concern for lay people. I have interviewed over three hundred lay people about the soul, and spoken to more than ten million more on television and radio talk shows. From a lay perspective, if we are whole and unified people, and there is no soul, then death of the body means total annihilation. If there is no personal survival of death, they reason, the implication is that Christ either didn't rise from the dead or doesn't care about them. When I try to explain that theologians say that our hope is the resurrection, they ask a logical question: What happens between death and resurrection? How profound! I have interviewed hundreds of clergy and theologians and asked them precisely that question. Many do not answer. Some assume—incorrectly—that the Bible doesn't deal with this issue. Many clergy tell me that they have never even thought about what happens to human beings immediately after death.

According to the apostle Paul, "We look not at what can be seen but at what cannot be seen; for what can be seen is temporary, but what cannot be seen is eternal" (2 Cor. 4:18). When many biblical scholars today emphasize that humans are "whole and unified," they are emphasizing that which can be seen (i.e., human nature prior to death) and ignoring that which cannot be seen (i.e., human nature immediately after death). In other words, the table is tilted in favor of a secular understanding of humans. "The soul of you is the whole of you," they say in seminaries.

Theologians often tell me that they have stopped talking to

lay people about the soul, because lay people are unwilling to hear that there is no soul-body dualism and no immortal soul. Such a comment always painfully reminds me of Jesus' assignment to Peter, "Feed my sheep" (John 21:17). I don't think Jesus meant that theologians should withhold from the sheep the kind of food that the sheep crave.

Although I believe the Protestant churches have a major problem surrounding the issue of the soul, what troubles me more deeply is the communication barrier between church leaders and lay people about this issue. I don't think the body of Christ works well if the leaders are no longer talking to lay people about something so important. When the shepherds go one way and the sheep a different way, the flock is left open to the attack of wolves (John 10:12). If theologians do want to talk with lay people about the soul, theologians will have to be humble enough to listen to lay people. There will need to be some give-and-take, an openness among Bible scholars to learn from "the least of these" brothers and sisters whom God has so often chosen as God's mouthpiece. The theologians might even learn something!

This book is an attempt to open that dialogue.

RECLAIMING
THE
SOUL

1

THE ORIGIN
OF THE SOUL

THE NATURE OF THE SOUL is closely connected with its origin and destiny. In this book I contend that human beings enter an intermediate state after death and prior to resurrection (see chapter 4), which requires that humans are dichotomous—the soul and body are temporarily separated at death. The inner person survives after the outer and visible person becomes a corpse. However, our final repose consists of being embodied after the resurrection.[1]

Likewise, the origin of the soul provides a clue to understanding what it is—and who we really are. In discussing the soul's origin, we need to begin with the common human experience of conception, lest we get lost in abstractions. The sperm and egg join, and the two halves of DNA combine to form a fertilized egg. The egg grows into a blastula, and then into an embryo attached to a placenta, which embeds in the uterine lining. Women who truly want to be pregnant may experience conception as a miracle; others, of course, may experience it as an annoyance. The embryo grows into a fetus, which eventually moves enough so the mother is aware of the life inside her. With a certain amount of pain and agony, the woman gives birth to a baby, the umbilical cord is cut, and the baby must either breathe on its own or die. There is something sacred and mysterious about the birth of a child. At birth the infant is totally helpless, and must depend on its parents for almost everything. It cannot even hold up its own head. Over the course of many years the child requires attention, affection, and nurturance from its parents, and slowly develops into an independent human being. During the dependent years the child is sometimes a blessing, sometimes an adorable monster, and sometimes a total pain to its frazzled parents. (On average, most children are adorable.) All this may seem obvious. Yet we dare not ignore this fundamental and common experience.

Another part of our common experience—at least among Christians—is Christ's teaching that we should seek to be like little children, that they are a model for how we will be in heaven. "Truly I tell you, unless you change and become like little children, you will never enter the kingdom of heaven" (Matt. 18:3). Christ has underscored the fact that children are special, adorable, trusting, open to life in a way that we wish we could be as adults. He even called his followers "children."

On the other hand, we don't always experience children as adorable. Sometimes a child will scream all night, obstinately refuse to eat, bite others, or insist on playing with the poisons stored beneath the sink. From experience we learn that the human tendency to rebel against all reason may have started with Adam and Eve, but it certainly includes our children. Children are not simply innocent. They are also fallen. The savage nature of children is evident in both temper tantrums and the yearning to do whatever is forbidden, whether it is climbing down dangerous stairs, playing with electric sockets, eating the dog food, splashing in the toilet water, or rushing into a street filled with speeding cars. What makes these things exciting to the child is that they are forbidden. (I once read an article in *Family Circle* magazine titled "It's Easier to Wear Fruit on Your Head Than to Feed It to a Baby." "So you want to learn patience?" the writer asked. "Spend a few hours with a small person who uses her tongue as a plow to push a whole load of oatmeal down her bib."[2])

Perhaps the most striking aspect of infants is their remarkable capacity to learn and grow. They even learn how to eat oatmeal. Thus, whatever we can say about the soul, we must emphasize its propensity to learn new things.

The Bible speaks of the origin of humans, although it does not specifically address the origin of the soul. For example, Sarah and Abraham gave birth to Isaac by the traditional method of lovemaking, conception, pregnancy, and birth. God had promised Abraham descendants as numerous as the stars of the sky, and he was granted a miracle—the miracle of fertility in old age. (According to the Bible Abraham was 100 years old, and Sarah was 90.) Yet there is no separate description of the origin of Isaac's soul.

The prophet Isaiah said it was God "who made you, who formed you in the womb" (Isa. 44:2, 24, 49:5; see also Job 31:15, Eccles. 11:5, Jer. 1:5). These passages indicate that God is involved in every aspect of human life, especially in the creation of babies in the womb. Jeremiah was foreknown by God even before conception: "Before I formed you in the womb I knew you" (Jer. 1:5). Although these verses indicate God's involvement, they do not speak of the origin of the soul as different from the origin of the body.

THREE THEORIES OF THE SOUL

Although the Bible does not discuss the origin of the soul, except for the traditional method of creating children, this topic was of great interest to the early church leaders such as Melito of Sardis, Origen, Macrina and Gregory of Nyssa, Tertullian, Jerome, Augustine, Pelagius, and Methodius of Olympus. Over the centuries the Christian tradition has formulated three theories regarding the soul:

• The *preexistent theory* holds that the soul exists eternally before birth, and enters the body of a fetus sometime during pregnancy. This view was held by Plato and Origen, but was formally discarded by the church as heresy. The Mormon church adopted the preexistent theory in the nineteenth century.

3

- The *creationist theory* holds that God creates each individual soul and attaches it to the body of the fetus sometime during pregnancy. The timing is disputed. Thomas Aquinas held that this occurs late in pregnancy, when the mother feels the baby moving. Today, the Catholic church teaches that "ensoulment" occurs at conception.

- The *traducianist theory* holds that the infant's soul derives from the father's soul. During lovemaking the man gives sperm to the woman, and also gives of his soul. Tertullian, a third-century theologian, based this idea on the following verse from scripture: "All the souls that came out of the loins of Jacob were seventy souls" (Exod. 1:5 KJV).[3] Proponents of the traducianist theory, such as Martin Luther, used this idea to explain how original sin is transmitted from generation to generation.

As we ponder these three theories, it is striking how abstract they are. Not only are they remote from the everyday experience of how we make children, but they are also remote from the Bible—which has, as I have suggested, remarkably little to say about the origin of the soul. The traducianist theory may actually appear to be biblical, because children and parents are so closely connected in the Bible that on occasion children were punished for the sins of the parents; according to the Old Testament, God "punishes the children for the sin of the fathers to the third and fourth generation" (Num. 14:18; Deut. 5:9). Later, however, punishment of the offspring was repudiated (Jer. 31:29–30; Ezek. 18:2–22).

The Bible repeatedly indicates that all the future generations are inside a man (the man's "seed"), like a box inside a box inside a box. (It is often hard to tell whether a name such as "Edom" refers to the father of the tribe or to the entire tribe— in this case, the Edomites. The name "Israel" refers sometimes to the patriarch Jacob and sometimes to all the Israelites.) The implication is that all the "seed" (i.e., all the souls who are offspring) come from the patriarch. This is most consistent with the traducianist theory of the origin of the soul—the theory that the soul of the child derives from the father.

A second striking feature of these theories is the degree to which the traducianist theory is male chauvinist. If the soul of a child comes from its parents, we would expect it to come from both parents, especially the mother. We now know that mothers contribute more to the formation of children than do fathers.

The third striking aspect of these traditional theories is that they leave us with the impression that the soul is static after it comes into existence. There is no emphasis on learning or on growth of the soul. Yet our experience of babies is that the capacity to learn and grow is fundamental to their existence.

The fourth striking aspect of these theories of the soul's origin is that they are related to the question of abortion. If the soul exists from conception, as the Roman Catholic church has maintained since the nineteenth century, abortion is murder and a violation of the Sixth Commandment.

All three traditional theories of origin were discussed in the days of the Roman Empire, when a drastic distinction was drawn between animate and inanimate objects. An *animus* was a soul, and it was what made something move from within— i.e., it "animated" the body (the Latin verb *animare* meant "to make alive"). There were two kinds of human bodies. A living body moved and therefore had a soul. A corpse was like any other composite object: it did not move, had no soul, and decomposed. Naturally this led theologians to speculate on precisely how this ethereal soul became attached to the physical body.

This is an interesting way of thinking, but it is remote from the kinds of questions and assumptions we have at the end of the twentieth century. We no longer have such radical dualism; it is a struggle for us to establish even a minimal soul-body dichotomy.

How should we think about this question in our time?

In chapter 4 we will describe the soul and body as being relatively merged early in life and growing more estranged as the person ages or grows chronically ill. Perhaps there is no discrepancy between the origin of the soul and the origin of the body. Yet at death the soul necessarily departs the body.

THE SOUL OF DNA

This way of thinking suggests that the soul and body do not have separate and unrelated origins. But where is the soul? Is there a soul unrelated to the egg, attached to it by some spiritual glue? This is what I call the "red balloon theory of the soul"—the notion that the soul is something peripheral like a balloon, not part of ordinary reality, attached to us by an ethereal string.

If one takes a *sacred* rather than a *secular* view of human nature, it is clear that humans are mysterious creatures. We cannot fully understand either ourselves or others. For example, the Bible tells us that the breath and image of God are inside us. This means that there are infinite mysteries hidden inside each person, even inside a fertilized egg. This is humbling; we should not think that we can truly understand what makes a human being.

I believe that the soul comes into existence at the time of conception. I also believe that our souls are partially intrinsic to our DNA, that our DNA has information about the soul written in it.

DNA has two qualities: a "body" and a "soul." DNA is like a scroll on which information is written. The scroll, as James Watson and Francis Crick discovered in 1953, is a double helix. Information written on a scroll has two aspects: the physical ink and the shape of the letters. In the case of DNA, the letters written in it consist of four bases (adenine, uracil, guanine, and cytosine). Each set of three letters is the name of one of twenty different amino acids. For example, the word "GAU" ("guanine-adenine-uracil") is the genetic code name of the amino acid we call aspartic acid.

The oldest written language on earth was written by God: the genetic code. It predates all other written languages: Sumerian cuneiforms, Egyptian hieroglyphs, Sanskrit, Chinese/

Japanese, Korean, Norwegian runes, Aztec, Proto-Elamite, and Semitic. Yet only recently did Watson and Crick figure out how to begin reading the language of DNA. During the second half of the twentieth century, geneticists have devoted themselves to reading and trying to decipher this most ancient of the sacred languages. In this language, God has described every aspect of every biological entity on earth.

On every sacred scroll, such as the Dead Sea Scrolls, there is a distinction to be made between the physical properties of the writing and its meaning. DNA is like every other scroll in this regard. For example, one might change one of the bases from uracil to cytosine, so that the physical writing is different. Instead of "GAU" the word would now be "GAC" ("guanine-adenine-cytosine"). Although such a change would result in the DNA having a different physical structure, the meaning would remain unchanged, for in either case the written word refers to aspartic acid.

Just as there is a difference between words and meaning in human language,[4] the same is true of DNA as a language. For example, several genes (i.e., several sequences of DNA) are required to make hemoglobin, the biological molecule that has been studied more than any other. There are many variations. Almost all the different forms of hemoglobin (each found in a different person) accomplish the same job with equal efficiency. The job is carrying oxygen inside the red blood cells. Thus, although there are many different descriptions of hemoglobin written in different people's DNA, they all have the same meaning.

The founder of modern linguistics, Noam Chomsky, has shown that in any language written words are different from their deeper meanings.[5] Sentences convey meaning, but individual words may vary and the sentence still convey the same meaning.

A semantic approach to individual words overlooks the essence of language, which is the concepts that are conveyed by whole sentences and paragraphs. James Barr showed that this was true of the Bible in his earth-shaking book *The Semantics of Biblical Language*.[6] It is also true of DNA.

For example, God designed the hemoglobin complex of four molecules in such a way that it can carry twenty times its volume in oxygen—a remarkably efficient system. There are many different ways of describing the hemoglobin molecule in DNA language, but most of the differences are unimportant because they do not result in a crippled hemoglobin molecule. Although sickle cell trait or some other genetic anomaly may produce an unacceptable form of hemoglobin, such diseases are minor by comparison with the robust variety found in healthy hemoglobin structure. Thus, one may vary the DNA words and still convey the same meaning: a highly efficient molecule for carrying oxygen in the blood.

It is important to distinguish between the forest and the trees. Biologists and geneticists can't talk about biological systems today without using language that conveys a sense of purpose. They say, "This DNA mutation occurred in order to . . ." or "The purpose of hemoglobin is to carry oxygen." In television programs on nature, constant reference is made to the purpose of salmon swimming upstream, the purpose of the human immune system, or the purpose of the front legs of Tyrannosaurus Rex. But how could hemoglobin, which has no mind, have a purpose? Whose purpose are they talking about, if not the Creator's?

For thousands of years, people have examined the biological world and concluded that it was designed with a purpose in mind. The assumption has been that God had a purpose in designing all the plants and animals. At the end of the twentieth century, biological researchers look at the biological world, and find themselves describing it in terms of purpose—but they stop there. They imagine that the random events of a purposeless universe could somehow have created a system with a purpose.

What's wrong with this picture? The problem is that these scientists deny the existence of a Creator but unwittingly accept the existence of a miracle. That miracle is inescapable but seldom acknowledged in every theory about how a purposeful biological system arose from the purposeless bumping about of inanimate molecules.

In her article "A Biological Perspective on Empathy," Leslie Brothers claims that empathy among people is embedded in the biological order of creation.[7] Yet, by sleight of hand, she establishes this claim without mentioning a Creator. She implies that empathy is part of human biology, which in turn arises from DNA.

But everywhere research scientists look today they see God's fingerprints. Every biological system was designed with a purpose in mind, although researchers stop short of saying whose mind conceived the purpose. All the scientific evidence today points to a purpose, but it is considered "unscientific" to say that there was a Creator. Scientists with faith may think God is behind it all, but they wouldn't say so in "scientific" discourse. My point is simple: that the purpose is conveyed in God's writing on the scrolls of DNA.

Returning to the fertilized egg, I claim that DNA is composed of two aspects: a physical aspect and a meaning. In this respect it is like all other written languages, as James Barr and Noam Chomsky have shown in their respective studies of human language. The fertilized egg contains two aspects embedded in the very core of the egg: the physical structure of the DNA could be called its body, and the meaning of the language written in the DNA could be called its spirit or soul.

There is no evidence that God creates new DNA each time an egg is fertilized. Half the DNA comes from the mother and half from the father. Therefore, the creationist theory of the origin of the soul has no support in science today. The biological evidence is that the information stored in the DNA of the sperm and egg makes a new baby, but God does not add any brand-new DNA information that comes neither from the sperm nor from the egg. (If God does add spiritual information not stored in DNA, that is outside the domain of science.)

The traducianist theory is strongly supported by molecular

researchers—provided that one major revision is made. Recall that Tertullian suggested that the soul of the baby comes from the soul of the father; clearly, however, the soul comes from both the mother and the father. Actually, the mother contributes a slight bit more to the formation of the baby than does the father, because, although the mother and father each contribute 23 chromosomes to the newborn, the DNA embedded in the mitochondria (which is a forty-seventh chromosome not often mentioned) comes only from the mother. Further, the soul of a baby gains further definition by early childhood experiences. Such experiences are primarily experiences involving the parents—especially the mother.

WHAT IS THE NATURE OF THE SOUL?

If the soul originates with the purpose or meaning of the language written in the DNA, what can we learn about the nature of that soul? In the first place, we learn that it is not just a rational or a philosophical soul. Christian theologians such as Gregory of Nyssa got on the wrong track here. The soul of DNA is like the soul described in the Bible: it is the life force, that which animates each and every cell of the human body, that which produces growth and controls all physiology.

There has been too much emphasis on the brain or mind as the locus of the soul. The brain may be a central focus of human nature, but the soul is found throughout the body. Even the ancient Christian theologians such as Tertullian and Augustine knew this, because they spoke of the vegetative soul that makes every aspect of our body alive. The soul exists before the brain exists.

To reiterate, first there is a fertilized egg, which divides and forms a blastula and then an embryo. During the first trimester of pregnancy there is an overproduction of neuronal material, so that the fetus enters the second trimester of pregnancy with too much brain material. In the second trimester, the brain is sculpted. Some cells are programmed to die, so as to give the brain more shape. Other cells migrate hither and yon. But fundamentally it is the soul that creates the brain. In other words, the DNA directs all this sculpting of the brain, for the purpose of producing a brain compatible with the human mind. That purpose—God's purpose—is what I am calling the soul.

If the soul is so deeply embedded in, or entangled with, the DNA, what happens if the fetus dies? We can only assume that the soul or spirit of the fetus survives, because Jesus said that we should "not despise one of these little ones; for, I tell you, in heaven their angels continually see the face of my Father in heaven" (Matt. 18:10). In other words, there is an angel in heaven, with direct access to God, corresponding to each baby.

But how could the soul survive the death of the body of a fetus? The answer is simple. If the DNA expresses a purpose, it is God's purpose—and surely God can survive the loss of the DNA and still have the same purpose. This theme repeats itself over and over: the soul exists because God exists, and the human mind exists because the soul exists.

At birth an infant has certain qualities that are the core characteristics of the soul. The infant is totally involved in a relationship with its parents, and cannot imagine existing separate from that relationship. Babies are completely dependent on and trusting of the parents. The only way for infants to survive and grow is by nurturance and affection from the parents. Babies don't experience themselves as separate, nor do they think of themselves as being independent identities; rather, they are part of their parents in a kind of fusion or merger. Babies exist in a pseudoeternity in the sense that they live in a timeless world, an "eternal now" in which yesterday and tomorrow don't exist.

Jesus said that "unless you change and become like little children, you will never enter the kingdom of heaven" (Matt. 18:3). The implication is that the open, trusting, and boundaryless quality of an infant's personality is what we should strive to emulate. Fifty years after birth a sophisticated person needs to struggle to rediscover what he or she knew at birth: that there is no independent existence apart from one's Parent, upon whom one must depend for nurturance. Without God we would not be able to take our next breath. Babies simply trust their parents to keep them alive, whereas we adults need to learn to trust God. In the newborn infant, we see the meaning and purpose that God wrote into the DNA. It is the God-given nature of our souls.

Identical twins have identical DNA. Such twins tend to have identical personalities. It is as if God had the same idea for two people. Studies have shown that identical twins raised in separate households turn out to be more exact copies of one another than identical twins raised in the same household.[8] This is because the DNA tends to produce the same personality disposition. When identical twins are raised in the same house, their parents and teachers make every effort to emphasize small differences between the children, because adults are uncomfortable with carbon copies. But when adults are not consciously trying to emphasize and produce differences, the two children living in separate houses tend to mature and blossom in identical ways.

After birth, the soul of a baby is profoundly influenced by its parents and early life experiences. But it is the newborn who shows us what the soul is like in its natural state, when the brain is only two-thirds formed. We find that the soul is so deeply involved with the body that it is impossible to draw a distinction between the two. There is no mind and body, just a baby. When the infant cries it does not mean that it has an unpleasant thought so much as it means gastric distress or an immature central nervous system.

When theologians refer to people as "embodied souls" they probably have in mind healthy young people, such as seminary students. A baby is a perfect example of what it means to be an embodied soul, for when you see the infant's body you see its soul. The soul has intrinsic properties, such as being trusting, needy, bewildered, seeking nurturance from the parents, and having an enormous capacity to grow and learn. Most babies are naturally oriented toward their parents, and so they receive the nourishment and affection needed for growth. Similarly, when an adult is oriented toward God, she or he receives the nourishment and affection needed for growth. But some babies do not respond to their parents, and those babies tend to die. (This is diagnosed as "failure to thrive." The oldest child I ever saw with this diagnosis was six years old but tiny in size, and had to be fed through a tube. Most such children die within a few months.)

The primary agenda of a fetus and of a baby is to grow. We cannot understand the soul without emphasizing—as did the early church leaders—that it originates as potential, not as fully developed or actualized. The soul engenders the growth of the body of a fetus in an orderly manner, including the growth and structuring of the brain. And, as I have said, the soul is remarkably capable of learning new information. Even the sprouting of nerve cells and the final structure of the brain are modified by the baby's experience.

I am proposing that biological systems serve a purpose—and that this purpose is an expression of both the soul and God's thinking. The purpose of a baby is to grow. The infant cannot survive on its own. It is designed (by God) for the purpose of expressing its needs in such a way as to mobilize the parents to meet those needs. Did you ever see parents when their baby is crying? They cannot sit still, nor can they close their ears, nor can they ignore the plaintive wailing. There is an inborn parental instinct, programmed into the deepest part of the parental soul, that drives the parent to seek relief from the agony of hearing a baby's cry. Sometimes milk is needed, sometimes a dry diaper or a cuddling hug, and sometimes the parent goes out of his or her mind and never learns why the baby continues to cry. Many mothers, responding to their babies' needs, spend years feeling exhausted and uncertain whether they are adequate as mothers.

The human soul is not designed to be an individual who is self-reliant and able to survive without others. The soul is not like the rational mind of a philosopher. Rather, the soul of a human, more than any other species, is designed to be dependent and interactive. In its earliest stages, the soul is primarily nonverbal, not the "rational soul" of which philosophers have spoken.

The New Testament speaks of two realities, one seen and the other unseen. The unseen reality, which is spiritual, is the more powerful and more decisive. When I spend any time with an infant, I find myself wondering whether perhaps the baby has more direct contact with the unseen world than I do. It probably does.

The soul of a baby has a certain power in terms of motivating adults to change and respond. I have friends who named their newborn "the little Ayatollah" in honor of his tyrannical control over the household. I have seen women quit their jobs and give up their careers because their babies need them more than they expected. I have seen couples get married for the sake of their babies. Babies are powerful little creatures, capable of creating families, capable of shaping the lives of adults to fit their own needs, capable of motivating a skirt-chasing father to give up adultery and devote himself to his family, capable of causing an elderly aunt to adopt a neglected baby niece whose mother was addicted to cocaine.

Of course, we dare not forget that children are also abused and neglected. This reminds us of their powerlessness and their utter dependence. I claim that the power and powerlessness of children are two sides of the same coin. The power of children comes out of the complete helplessness of the infant, for their powerlessness motivates adults to protect them. For example, other adults are motivated to intervene if a child is being abused or neglected.

A CASE HISTORY

The following case history regarding Dr. Alan Broadhead, a psychiatrist and ordained minister, illustrates how a soul can be shaped by early childhood experiences.[9]

Broadhead grew up as an only child in an atheist household

in rural poverty near Manchester, England. His father was a white-collar worker. Timid and meek elsewhere, his father was tyrannical and domineering at home. Alan's father was not physically abusive, but he would scream for hours at his wife and child. Loud contentiousness was the usual form of communication at home. Alan's father and mother lived in a destructive symbiotic relationship.

His mother never worked outside the house. She was a woman with an abysmal self-regard throughout her life. If we were to meet this woman, within three minutes she would introduce the idea that she had been found as a baby sitting in a gutter, abandoned by her "real" mother. The shame of being illegitimate tortured her. As a reflection of the emotional squalor inside her, as an adult she kept her house filthy, with thick dust and dirt over everything, and stacks of moldy dishes in the sink. When Alan later worked as a doctor, he made thousands of house calls, and only in one or two of those houses did he ever see more filth than what he had grown up with. He was not taught to wash or bathe. His clothes were wrinkled and smelly. Neither manners nor social graces were taught to Alan at home.

"A neglected or abused child holds onto the hope that someday his parents will give him some affection," Alan told me. "It is not a hope based on experience. It is a hope based on fantasy. If the child doesn't have that hope, then the child has nothing at all. On the basis of such hope I was intensely loyal to my parents."

Alan's family had no friends or social life. He carefully avoided telling anyone outside how bad it was at home. Later he discovered that the neighbors all knew. His family was notorious in the neighborhood. Occasionally Alan's paternal grandfather would visit and show interest in Alan. But for the most part, he had no nurturance or caring during the first four years of his life.

He spent most of his time in solitude, and grew comfortable with introverted fantasies. Loving nature, he hiked across the fields and collected bugs and mice. His fantasy life and reveries managed to remain a healthy part of his life, allowing him to survive childhood and giving him a rich imagination as an adult. He now thinks that under circumstances of such severe deprivation and abuse, a child simply either makes it or fails to make it. This is not based on any decision on the part of the child. It is a matter of the child's constitution, perhaps a genetically determined characteristic.

Alan remembers vividly the reveries he engaged in while playing alone in the fields as a child. "I have been overwhelmed at times by the majesty of the sea, and the sky, and the sun," he told me. "It is almost pantheistic. I love the Song of Creation from the *Hymnal.*"[10]

"Did you have that sense of reverie from the earliest part of your life?" I asked.

"Yes," he said. "From as far back as I can remember."

"Well, where on earth did that originate?" I asked. "You had a pretty awful mother. How could you have this experience of bonding with nature? Did you bond with your mother? Was she the original prototype of Mother Nature? Was your mother nurturant?"

"I have no idea if my mother was nurturant," he replied. "It is not something that I ever remember. On the other hand, the bonding between infant and mother can occur the other way around also. I was a possession of my mother's, like a toy. When I was an infant, I brought joy into her life. As I grew older, she had trouble accepting my independence. She had a hard time giving up breast-feeding me. My independence was not welcome. So I suppose from the earliest months of my life, before I began to get independent, she was nurturant. As I grew older, I lived in terror of this wretched woman. But I always longed for her also."

"She was so tormented," I said. "But I remember what you said about her finding peace in senility in her old age."

"In the last six months of her life," Alan said, "she finally found the serenity which had eluded her all her life. In the eighth

16

decade of life she became demented. Finally, she forgot the bitterness of being an illegitimate child. People said she looked like an angel, she was so tranquil. I wondered if maybe I caught a glimpse then of the angelic mother I knew during the first six months of my life."

"Did you internalize these parents?" I asked him.

"These parent imagos," he said. "Yes. I used to have a punitive and tyrannical superego. That superego came from internalizing my parents. I felt worthless, unacceptable. Only after I went through seven years of psychoanalysis did I come to see what Paul was talking about when he spoke of 'justification by faith alone.' Before psychoanalysis, when I was in seminary, I thought I was justified by good works. I had a primitive superego type of religion. My ability to feel OK based on faith alone was cemented by psychoanalysis. Before psychoanalysis I was dreadfully depressed, sometimes for months at a time. For decades I had a deep inner sense of worthlessness, and intense feelings of rage. I was terribly insecure and shy."

"Were your parents internalized entirely as 'bad parents?'" I asked. "Was there anything positive they gave you?"

"I had a powerful longing for my parents," he replied. "For years I didn't recognize it. Only when I got into psychoanalysis did I realize how much I longed for them. It was why I got so depressed. Like seeing my dad at the end of a long lane. 'Daddy, daddy, daddy,' I would shout, and run down the lane to greet him. Of course, my longing for my father would be destroyed almost immediately by the stupidity of his behavior."

The good internalized parents for Alan are the fantasy parents, the caring parents he wished he had, but didn't. It is sad.

It would be reasonable to expect that a child like Alan wouldn't have amounted to anything. What happened?

Alan's parents were intensely ambitious for him. They wanted him to achieve everything they had failed to achieve. Never did they go to church, nor were they in any way religious. But for some reason they wanted Alan to join the local church.

There was a mission church in a barn at the other end of the country lane on which they lived. When Alan was four, his parents told him that he should go up to the mission church and see what it was like. They did not offer to go with him. If he didn't like it, he need never go back again, they said. So he wandered up the street, a filthy and smelly four-year-old, and found his way into the barn. What greeted him there was an experience that changed his life permanently.

It was the Feast of the Harvest, the British equivalent of Thanksgiving. He wandered into a place filled from wall to wall with fragrant food, home-baked bread and pies, fresh flowers, music, gaiety, and a festive spirit. This being farm country, the Feast of the Harvest was a major feast day. He was welcomed and loved. He adored it. It was like the beginning of real life for him. Suddenly, he had discovered life outside the miserable confines of his home. This little mission church had no minister. Lay readers led the worship services. Once a month, a minister from outside would come by. By other people's standards it was a provincial, backwater, poverty-stricken, tiny place. But for Alan, it became his new home base and the center of his emotional life.

Adults in the church became surrogate parents to Alan. They loved him by virtue of their faith, and by virtue of their membership in the church. For example, there was a man who ran the youth group, which consisted of eight or nine kids. This man, Richard Whitehouse, was not well educated and was a supervisor at a factory. But he would ride his bicycle nine miles through all kinds of weather in order to be there to run the church group, and Alan could absolutely rely on the fact that he would be there, no matter what the weather. It was an impressive demonstration of commitment that was incredibly important to Alan. He learned he could rely on Richard Whitehouse in a way that he had been unable to rely on his parents.

"I sometimes wonder if I would have been such a devoted Christian," Alan said, "if life had been pleasant at home. The church wouldn't have been such a lifesaver had I not been drowning. For example, the other day I was telling my son that he was lucky he didn't have the hard life I had when I was his age. My son said, 'If you really want us to appreciate life, dad, you would have to beat the s—— out of us and pretend you don't like us.'"

"You have told me," I said, "that the little mission church in the barn was your 'saving grace.'"

"I internalized the church as my positive parents," Alan replied. "It was because it was right down the street. Had I been raised in Palestine, there would have been a mosque down the street, and I would have internalized the mosque. I would have become a devout Moslem. That is why I think that Christians and Jews, Moslems and Buddhists are equal. It all depends what is down the street."

"Did you internalize Richard Whitehouse?" I asked.

"Yes, he became part of my hagiography, one of the saints whose name is carved in my mind. I call these internalized people imagos. Fortunately, the people I met were those who cared about other people. Richard Whitehouse really cared about others, and not just to serve his own self-interest. So I internalized people like him. Therefore, I learned to care about other people. It is why I am not just the solitary, schizoid person I was during the first four years of my life. If I had been Oliver Twist I might have internalized Fagin, and then I would have grown up to be a thief. By God's grace the people I met as a child were caring, and not Fagin.

"The only outside speakers who ever came to this out-of-the-way corner of the earth," Alan continued, "were missionaries from China and Africa and other exotic places. They would bring fanciful clothes for us kids to try on. They talked about places that were very different than this little farming village which was my whole experience. My imagination would soar. I began to formulate a plan. I wanted to be a minister because I wanted to give something to the church, in exchange for all that the church had given me. And specifically I wanted to be a missionary, and go to someplace fabulous and exotic. To this end I thought it might be neat to become a doctor, a medical missionary."

Alan did become a doctor, a medical missionary, in an exotic place: North Dakota.

2

THE LOSS
OF THE SOUL

I<small>T IS NO ACCIDENT</small> that the soul is missing at the turn of the millennium: during the first half of the twentieth century, biblical theologians and philosophers worked hard to get rid of it. Krister Stendahl, a leading New Testament scholar at Harvard Divinity School, has written:

> The question about immortality of the soul is interesting for someone who is primarily a biblical scholar because he specializes in sixty-six so-called books that do not know of the immortality of the soul. . . . The whole world that comes to us through the Bible, Old Testament and New Testament, is not interested in the immortality of the soul. And if you think it is, it is because you have read this into the material. . . .
>
> The whole concern for individual identity, which is the technical meaning of immortality of the soul, is not to be found in the Good Book because its concern and focus is elsewhere. . . . The question is not: What is going to happen to little me? Am I to survive with my identity or not? The question is rather whether God's justice will win out. . . . An increasing number of men and women are less and less concerned about the immortality of the soul, especially their own.[1]

And C. G. Berkouwer wrote:

> Scripture never pictures man as a dualistic, or pluralistic being, but . . . in all its varied expressions the whole man comes to the

fore. The discussion has especially turned on this point, whether the term "soul" as used in Scripture has some special religious emphasis in the sense that we must deduce at least some sort of dichotomy. And this is more and more denied by theologians. . . . [The soul] may not be made the special seat of religion, in dichotomistic and anthropological fashion, since religion deals precisely with the relation of the whole man with God.[2]

Finally, Reinhold Niebuhr, the greatest American theologian of this century, also rejected the soul. Niebuhr wrote that there are

two distinctive views of man: (a) The view of classical antiquity, that is of the Graeco-Roman world, and (b) the Biblical view. It is important to remember that while these two views are distinct and partly incompatible, they were actually merged in the thought of medieval Catholicism. . . .

Modern culture has thus been a battleground of two opposing views of human nature. . . .

[Soul-body] dualism has the consequence for the doctrine of man of identifying the body with evil and of assuming the essential goodness of mind or spirit. This body-mind dualism and the value judgments passed upon both body and mind stand in sharpest contrast to the Biblical view of man and achieved a fateful influence in all subsequent theories of human nature. The Bible knows nothing of a good mind and an evil body. . . .

Christian thought [allows] an appreciation of the unity of body and soul in human personality. . . .

In Hebrew thought the soul of man resides in his blood and the concept of an immortal mind in a mortal body remains unknown to the end.[3]

At Yale University, the primary opposition to the soul would not be found in the medical school. Neither the department of psychiatry nor that of psychology has much to say about the soul. They certainly don't speak against it. The primary opposition to the soul at Yale would be located in the divinity school.[4]

When I began to write about the soul, I was troubled that the word had been largely removed from twentieth-century translations of the Bible (see below), compared with the King James Version. Trying to understand that, I phoned my neighbor, Professor Brevard S. Childs (known as Barton), who teaches Old Testament at Yale. He told me that I should avoid the word "soul," because it was a Platonic word that implied a soul-body dualism not found in the Bible. He was quite gracious, and had me over for tea, while he explained why the soul was not a biblical concept.

After that I talked about the soul with hundreds of other biblical scholars, most of whom either hated the word and said it was unbiblical, or knew that the official party line was an anti-soul position. This troubled me so deeply that I joined several theological scholarly societies so I could try to understand how biblical scholars thought.

When I asked my former teacher Krister Stendahl, an internationally known scholar who wrote *The School of Saint Matthew*,[5] why the word "soul" was found so infrequently in twentieth-century translations of the Bible, he started out with the same message I had heard from Barton Childs: that the word "soul" should be avoided. However, he and I began discussing my work as a psychiatrist, and eventually he agreed that we need the word "soul" in order to understand the secular mental health movement from a theological perspective.[6]

In this chapter I explain why so many seminary professors, especially Bible scholars, are skittish about the soul. I briefly discuss four groups of thinkers: Protestant, Catholic, and Jewish theologians, and secular philosophers.

PROTESTANT THEOLOGIANS

Between 1926 and 1958 the central leaders of Protestantism turned against, attacked, and rejected soul-body dualism as being unbiblical. After about 1958 it was assumed that the war had been won.[7] Since then, only one noted New Testament scholar, C. J. De Vogel, has defended soul-body dualism as biblical.[8]

The biblical theology movement led the crusade against the soul. They made two assumptions, both of which were hostile to the soul. First, they assumed that Greek philosophical ideas were not found in the Bible, but were added to Christianity by church fathers such as Augustine. Plato had taught that the soul is inherently immortal.[9] Plato's ideas influenced early Christian theologians such as Tertullian, Origen, Gregory of Nyssa, and Augustine.[10]

Oscar Cullmann wrote a highly influential book, published in 1958, in which he denounced the intrinsic immortality of the soul as being a Greek philosophical idea derived from Plato, which he said was totally incompatible with the New Testament emphasis on resurrection of the dead.[11] Cullmann's ideas were extremely well received by biblical scholars. After Cullmann, many scholars, perhaps a majority, said that the New Testament didn't mention immortality but spoke of resurrection instead.[12]

It came to be accepted dogma that the Bible assumes an allegedly Hebrew concept of the whole, unified person throughout both the Old and New Testaments. Werner Jaeger wrote that soul-body dualism was a bizarre idea invented by Plato, found nowhere in the Bible, and imported as a contaminant into Christianity by the church fathers such as Augustine.[13] He also wrote that this immortal soul, which he and his scholarly colleagues had decided to reject, was "one of the foundations of Western civilization."

The biblical theology movement drew a drastic distinction between the allegedly "Greek" and "Hebrew" concepts of human nature. The Greek view involved the soul and was rejected as "unbiblical." The Hebrew concept was that no soul-body distinction could be made in the Bible, that humans were portrayed in a holistic manner. Resurrection of the body was said to be the biblical view of the afterlife.

Members of the biblical theology movement made a second

assumption that was equally hostile to the soul. They assumed that the Bible could be fully understood by studying the semantics and meaning of each individual word in the Bible. Gerhart Kittel produced a twelve-volume encyclopedia called the *Theological Dictionary of the New Testament,* which attempted an exhaustive definition of each individual word in the New Testament.

Word studies of terms such as "body," "soul," "heart," "spirit," and "flesh" further convinced biblical scholars that there was no soul-body dualism in the Bible.[14] For example, through the figure of speech called "synecdoche," these words could refer sometimes to a part of the person and sometimes to the whole person. When the King James Version says, "All the souls that came out of the loins of Jacob were seventy souls" (Exod. 1:5) and "We were in all in the ship two hundred three-score and sixteen souls" (Acts 27:37), the word "souls" is being used to refer to the whole person.

Further, a word such as "heart" could take on both spiritual and physical meanings, referring to the essence of a person, the location of thought, or the organ beating in one's chest. For these reasons, it became established dogma that the Bible did not allow one to construct a psychological or physiological picture of human nature, because all the parts and pieces were scrambled together like an omelet. Rather, the biblical emphasis was said to be on the relationship of the whole person to God.[15]

When a word-study technique is used, there are only a few verses in the Bible in which body and soul are clearly separate from each other. In Matthew 10:28 Jesus says we should not fear those who can kill the body but not the soul. According to I. H. Marshall, most Bible experts find this verse embarrassing and would prefer to sweep it under the rug.[16]

Soul-body dualism is also found in Philippians 1:23–24. De Vogel made a careful word study of that passage and showed that the "person-as-a-whole" theme is absent. The passage portrays clear duality, because Paul would prefer to leave his body and be with God. Thus Paul said he was made of two parts.

De Vogel concluded that the "person-as-a-whole" theme is the twentieth-century secular view of human nature, which has been erroneously read into the Bible by New Testament scholars.[17]

In the antisoul climate among biblical scholars, it became popular to say that the Hebrew word *nephesh* often did not refer to the soul. It referred to the throat, to life, to a personal pronoun, or to almost anything other than "soul."[18] Translators tried to clarify the situation by removing most occurrences of the term "soul." Not counting the Apocrypha, the word is found in the King James Version 533 times. It is found less often in twentieth-century translations: Revised Standard Version, 220 times; New Revised Standard Version, 180 times; New International Version, 136 times; and the Living Bible, 88 times.

One Bible translator said to me, "We think it is better, wherever possible, to use a word other than 'soul' to translate the Hebrew word *nephesh* or the Greek word *psyche* into English."[19]

Word studies proved hostile to the soul, because it appeared that an allegedly "Hebraic" concept of the whole, unified, and unsplittable human was found throughout both testaments.[20] This was based on the meanings in Greek of anthropological words such as *bios, dianoia, kardia, nous, pneuma, psuche, sarx, seautou, soma, zao,* and *zoe,* and the equivalent Hebrew terms in the Old Testament.[21]

James Barr showed that the semantics of biblical language does not hinge on the study of individual words, but on concepts.[22] Barr's criticism helped demolish biblical theology as a movement, but the word-study approach to anthropology persisted nevertheless. Most scholars ignored Barr's recent book defending the immortal soul.[23]

John Cooper has studied the problem of soul-body dualism in depth in his book *Body, Soul, and Life Everlasting: Biblical Anthropology and the Monism-Dualism Debate.* He adopts a position that he calls "holistic dualism," which states that humans are unified and whole during this life but come apart at death; the New Testament shows, he claims, that the spirit/soul goes into an intermediate state between death and bodily resurrection.[24] We will examine this issue in depth in chapter 4.

The water molecule provides an excellent model for what the Bible says about the nature of human beings. During this life the oxygen and hydrogen atoms are so merged that they share the same cloud of electrons. Thus one could say that there is a holistic or unified water molecule. But if the water molecule is broken apart, the oxygen can go one way and the hydrogen another way, so that we could say that the water molecule is a dichotomy.

Millard Erickson and John Cooper appear to be at opposite ends of the spectrum concerning soul-body dualism. Erickson emphasizes the unity ("conditional unity" or "contingent monism") of humans.[25] Cooper emphasizes dualism ("holistic dualism"). Yet, astonishingly, both scholars cite the water molecule as a good model for understanding what the Bible says about human nature. Erickson emphasizes the unity of the hydrogen and oxygen in a water molecule, which is to say he emphasizes human nature during this life. Cooper emphasizes the dichotomy of the hydrogen and oxygen in a water molecule, which is to say, he emphasizes human nature in the intermediate state after death and prior to resurrection.

The water molecule allows us to see that the experts agree on what the Bible says, but disagree on how to use that information for apologetic purposes. The Bible says that humans, like water molecules, are whole and unified during this life, but are so constructed that they come apart at death. One substance is called the body; the other substance is invisible.

So why is there such a huge debate on soul-body dualism in theology? It is simply a question of whether theologians prefer to emphasize this life or to emphasize what happens immediately after death. Those, like Millard Erickson, who strongly emphasize the unified nature of humans are biased in favor of this life. Those, like John Cooper, who strongly emphasize the two parts of humans are biased in favor of life after death. Erickson's approach provides no way to combat the destructive effects of the secular mental health movement, which also emphasizes this life. Cooper's approach provides ammunition for the church to use in defending itself against the invading army of secular psychotherapists.

Christians cannot simply hoist up the white flag and surrender to the secular psychotherapists. The secular concept is that we are nothing more than our bodies, and when our bodies die, we are annihilated forever. Although Erickson's position is not quite this secular, the average reader would have a hard time telling the difference. Many clergy I have interviewed think that the Christian message about human nature is the same as the secular psychotherapy message.

This is a tricky subject, as I have learned from debates with hundreds of biblical scholars and theologians. Talking about "dualism" is like walking across a mine field. We need to draw a distinction between the vocabulary of philosophers and that of theologians. From a philosophical point of view it is correct to say that biblical anthropology consists of "interactive dualism," which is proved by the fact that the entire human being is not 100 percent annihilated when the body dies. There is a corpse and something else, which is to say there are two parts. The word "dualism" simply means dichotomy in terms of ontologic substances. The word "interactive" means that body and soul are in close and cooperative communication during this life.

However, theologians don't talk much to philosophers. Theologians take the word "dualism" to mean something entirely different. To them the word implies Plato, which is to say a disparaging view of the body and an overvaluation of the soul, because they have been so strongly influenced by the antisoul crusade in theology.

I find it necessary to avoid the phrase "holistic dualism" when I talk with theologians and biblical scholars in order to avoid miscommunication. "Dualism" is a word that can be used in discussing anthropology with Christian philosophers, but when talking with biblical scholars I use "duality" or "dichotomy" to decrease the risk of miscommunication. But Protestant theologians are often so opposed to the soul that miscommunication occurs anyway.

One might think that a total reversal of Christian doctrine would require a vote of the ruling bodies of the various denominations. The church made a U-turn from the nineteenth-century emphasis on the salvation of souls as the central message of Christianity to the twentieth-century teaching that the soul is a non-Christian idea. You might think that a world convocation would be called to debate the pros and cons of such a doctrinal reversal. However, in the case of the soul, no ruling body of any denomination has ever debated the idea of discarding the soul. Biblical scholars made that decision on their own. They didn't consult anyone else. Nor did they consider how such a drastic change would affect the lay people. To make matters worse, the radical change in direction of Christian doctrine isn't even acknowledged in most textbooks of theology. The authors pretend that they are presenting "that old-time religion." You have to read between the lines to realize that they simply forgot to mention the absence of the soul.

What is a common-sense approach? It starts by asking what happens to me when I die.

In my interviews of 248 theologians and clergy, I asked this question: What happens between death and bodily resurrection? One-third of Episcopal clergy and 17 percent of United Methodist clergy said they had absolutely no idea. Many of them said they had never thought about the question. Some said (erroneously) that the Bible is silent on that subject. Some said they dodge that question when kids ask it. One clergyman said he lies at funeral services and at the graveyard, assuring the relatives that the deceased is now with Christ, while he is completely unsure where the deceased might be, perhaps dead in the grave until the resurrection.

In addition to the large number of liberal Protestant clergy who say "I don't know," about 7 percent say they are sure that the dead are "asleep" in the grave, that there is no conscious existence between death and bodily resurrection. One Episcopal minister said, "I am terribly orthodox about this. We will be asleep after we die. There will be no consciousness. That is the orthodox viewpoint." Another minister said he didn't believe in life after death; he thought that Christianity works better without that doctrine.

Almost all the Protestant clergy who thought the dead were unconscious (i.e., "soul sleep," as many Adventist churches teach) indicated that they are cautious and hide their views from lay people, since the laity don't agree and get quite upset if they hear that view.

My own view, expressed throughout this book, but especially in chapter 4, is that the Bible is clear that there is an intermediate state of conscious existence between death and bodily resurrection. But this is not what is emphasized in Protestant seminaries. During theological training most Protestant clergy learn some variation of the following:

1. Soul-body dualism is found nowhere in the Bible. It is a false teaching from the Greeks. The alleged Hebrew view found in the Bible is that humans are whole and cannot be split into body and soul.

2. The New Testament hope is for resurrection of the person, not immortality of the soul. Immortality of the soul is a false teaching from the Greeks, and is not compatible with the alleged Hebrew view of the whole person found in the Bible.

These two teachings are central to the thinking of many Protestant clergy, according to my surveys. In my view they are slogans that prevent us from thinking clearly about biblical anthropology. (For a more extensive discussion of exactly what the Bible does say, see my article "One's Self-Concept and Biblical Theology."[26]) In chapter 4 I will defend the concept of an intermediate state of existence between bodily death and bodily resurrection.

Logically, if the biblical view is that there is never a split between body and soul, and the body dies, then the soul also dies. One scholar stated the problem eloquently: "Professor Cullmann inferred that Jesus did not believe in immortality of the soul; that to him death meant the death of both body and soul; and hence that resurrection, in which he explicitly expresses a belief, meant to him a new creation of soul as well as body."[27] I will show in chapter 4 that this is a misreading of Cullmann, who actually endorsed an intermediate state, and therefore had an apparent contradiction in his own thinking.[28]

John Cooper wrote that if New Testament scholars were correct in what they say in denouncing all forms of soul-body dichotomy and rejecting the immortal soul, then "what millions of Christians believe will happen to them when they die [would be] a delusion."[29] Do Protestant Bible experts actually follow their ideas to the logical conclusion that there is total annihilation when we die and that God re-creates us ex nihilo when we are resurrected? I did a computer search of the *Theological Abstracts* between 1955 and the present, and I was unable to find a single biblical professor who is willing to defend this "annihilation/re-creation" view. Thus the logical conclusion one would reach based on the two teachings noted above is not a view that any scholars of the Bible are willing to defend. This suggests that there is a contradiction somewhere.

At a time when the laity need leadership concerning the questions "Who am I?" and "What will become of me and my loved ones when we die?", many Protestant clergy tell me they avoid talking with lay people about these issues.

ROMAN CATHOLIC THEOLOGIANS

The position of Roman Catholic theologians about the soul is more nuanced than the views of Protestant and Jewish theologians. To some extent the Roman Catholic church has been affected by the strong hostility to the soul found among biblical scholars. This is evident, for example, in the *New Dictionary of Theology*, which discusses the 436 most important topics in Catholic theology, but there is absolutely no discussion of the soul. The listing under "Soul" refers the reader elsewhere: "See Anthropology, Christian." In that section the word "soul" is never mentioned, nor is it found under the heading "Immortality."[30]

On the other hand, the Roman Catholic church has been somewhat protected from the antisoul winds of the twentieth century for two reasons. First, the church's official theologian, Thomas Aquinas, defined the soul as the form of the body, following Aristotle.[31] That definition is less open to being attacked as "dualistic" by Bible scholars. Second, the Roman Catholic church has a tradition of making slow and thoughtful decisions about major doctrinal changes. The turn against the soul during the twentieth century, while sweeping through Protestantism like a tornado, was greeted with careful, measured analysis in Roman Catholicism.

The traditional Roman Catholic interpretation holds that during this life there is no soul-body dualism because the soul is the "form" of the body. After death, the soul is instantly immortal and is judged by God in a prompt manner. In my survey of fifty-four Catholic priests, I found that almost all of them still maintain this view. They are aware that the soul-body dispute is a major problem in the Protestant churches, but Catholic priests don't experience a similar contradiction in Catholic doctrine.

The Catholic church adopted as its official position that the soul is the substantial form of the body.[32] Thus, soul and body are of one nature, not two. Etienne Gilson, a modern Thomistic scholar, indicates that the soul receives the body into communion with itself. For these reasons it is difficult to imagine how the soul could separate from the body at death, and this is viewed as a mystery in Catholic theology and philosophy.[33] The composite human being is dissolved at death.[34] One explanation of what happens when the soul is disembodied (between death and resurrection) is that the soul is not able to organize the dead body, and regains its ability to organize the body only at the resurrection.[35]

The Second Vatican Council emphasized the unity of body and soul.[36] The unity of body and soul is again underlined in the 1994 *Catechism of the Catholic Church*:

The unity of the soul and body is so profound that one has to consider the soul to be the "form" of the body; i.e., it is because of the spiritual soul that the body made of matter becomes a living, human body; spirit and matter, in man, are not two natures united, but rather their union forms a single nature.[37]

The *Catechism* also states:

Man, though made of body and soul, is a unity. . . . For this reason man may not despise his bodily life. Rather he is to regard his body as good and to hold it in honor since God has created it and will raise it up on the last day.[38]

Aquinas said that the soul is the first principle of life in all living things.[39] He adopted the traditional distinction among vegetative, sensitive, and intellectual souls.[40] All plants and animals have a vegetative soul, which is their physiological ability to live and grow. Animals, but not plants, have a sensitive soul, the sensory ability to know and respond to the environment. But only humans have a rational soul (which includes within itself a vegetative and sensitive soul). The rational soul is said to have two principal faculties, intellect and will, according to Catholic philosophy. [41]

Although there is a history of friendly collaboration between Catholic priests and mental health professionals, the literature does not provide a discussion of whether such professionals treat the Catholic soul—and if they do not treat the soul, what aspect of theological anthropology do they treat?[42] (Theological anthropology is that part of theology that concerns human nature, *anthropos* being the Greek word for "human.") For example, if the traditional soul has only two faculties (intellect and will), where do emotions and personality, dreams, introjects (internal objects), family relationships, and unconscious conflicts lie? If the soul is "rational" according to Aquinas, how do we classify the "irrational" aspects of humans? Are they part of the soul or not? Aquinas' view of the soul does not leave much room for incorporating emotional and psychological aspects.

The ambiguous position of the Catholic church vis-à-vis the soul is evident in my field research. I did a random telephone survey of every eighth Catholic priest in the Archdiocese of Hartford, Connecticut, achieving a response rate of 93 percent. I interviewed fifty-four priests about the soul, which was a statistically representative sample of the entire archdiocese.

Ninety-six percent of the parish priests thought the soul was essential to the Catholic religion, to the point that there could be no Christianity without a doctrine of the soul. One said, "There would be no Christian religion, no gospel, without the soul, which lives forever." Yet only 57 percent used the word much. One subject said, "The soul has been underemphasized; it is time to reemphasize it."

In another survey, I studied the attitudes of 135 Catholic lay people toward the soul. Although almost all of them thought the soul was essential to their religion, many of them told me that they had not heard the word "soul" mentioned in homilies in church, nor had they read about the soul in their Christian education.

One might conclude that the soul may still be present in Catholic churches to a greater extent than in Protestant churches or Protestant Bibles, but it is not emphasized.

JUDAISM

The soul crashed on the Protestant Theological Stock Exchange, and lost some of its value in Catholicism. Now I will turn to the almost total loss of the immortal soul from Judaism.

The absence of the immortal soul is so much taken for granted in mainstream Judaism that the challenge is for anyone to assert that this is unusual. Most Christians today assume that Judaism is, and always has been, a religion focused on this life, promoting ethics and right living. It comes as a surprise that Jewish theologians such as Simcha Paull Raphael and Dan Cohn-Sherbok assert that the immortal soul was central to Judaism prior to Auschwitz.

The soul, and its survival of death, was a central part of Judaism in every century for thousands of years. Since the Holocaust, however, it has been said that the immortal soul is missing from mainstream Judaism 364 days a year and is found in the synagogue only during the *Yizkor* service, when the souls of the six million Jews exterminated by the Nazis are commemorated. (It is also found among certain minority sects, such as the Hasidim, and in mystical Judaism, such as the Kabbalah.[43]) In *The Jewish Way in Death and Mourning*, Marucice Lamm dismisses the afterlife as something about which a living Jew can know essentially nothing.[44]

In the fourth book of Maccabees there is a vivid description of persecution by King Antiochus IV of Syria, who attempted to destroy the Jewish religion by forcing Hebrews to eat pork and renounce God in the year 170 B.C.E. When they refused, Antiochus took a family of seven brothers and tortured them, pulling their arm and leg joints apart, chopping off their limbs, burning them with fire, and eventually murdering them. Then he killed the mother. All eight were faithful to God, and refused to eat pork, preferring death. The story is even carried today in the Catholic Bible (New Jerusalem Bible), in 2 Maccabees 7. Antiochus subjected the Jews to what the Jews have always been subject to: pogroms. The fourth book of Maccabees is an inspiring and uplifting book, because it emphasizes the triumph of the seven brothers over the savage king in the afterlife, where their spirits are immortal and instantly rewarded by God.

Rabbi Aaron Berachia ben Moses of Modena published his book *Ma'avo Yabok* in 1626. This book expounds the adventures of the immortal soul after death; it is somewhat akin to a Jewish version of the *Tibetan Book of the Dead*. It has been widely read for three hundred years by both Ashkenazic and Sephardic Jews in Central and Eastern Europe. But it has never been translated into English.[45]

As Dan Cohn-Sherbok suggests, Judaism has largely moved from a traditional belief in the immortality of the soul to a contemporary emphasis on this life.[46]

SECULAR PHILOSOPHERS

We have described the loss of the soul from Judaic and Protestant theology, and the decreased emphasis on the soul in Catholic theology. In a parallel development, the mind or "I" has disintegrated and has been lost from modern philosophy. This is described in detail in William Barrett's *Death of the Soul: From Descartes to the Computer.*[47]

The watershed thinker in the development of modern philosophy was Immanuel Kant, who established the basic assumptions that have prevailed ever since. Kant's work did not emphasize the person who observed the universe. There was no substance called the "soul."

Post-modern philosophy is as fragmented into unrelated specialties that don't talk to one another as is everything else in the intellectual world today. But there is one assumption that is agreed upon by all schools of philosophy: that there is no substance called the "soul." Generally they don't like the idea of substances at all.

Existentialists such as Martin Heidegger and Jean-Paul Sartre speak of human experience and freedom but not of any coherent entity providing a core to that experience and freedom. Analytical philosophers such as Bertrand Russell and Ludwig Wittgenstein analyze logic or language but make no reference to a coherent mind as the core or source of that logic or language. Alfred North Whitehead's philosophy makes everything psychical rather than physical, but Whitehead did not emphasize the individual mind or allow a distinction between body and soul. And computers have given rise to a form of processing that cognitive psychologists have taken as the model for how the human brain works.

What is missing from modern philosophy is the "I," a coherent person at the core of it all. One way of summarizing this phenomenon would be to say that secular philosophy is hostile to, or denies the existence of, the central core of what makes us human. Karl Popper and John Cooper stand out among twentieth-century philosophers as the primary defenders of the soul-body interactive dualism.[48]

SECULAR PSYCHOTHERAPY

The common theme throughout this chapter, in our discussion of Protestant and Jewish theologians and secular philosophers, is that most scholars have adopted a secular view of human nature. Neither theologians nor philosophers are providing ordinary people with what they have traditionally provided—a discussion of the soul—and my experience is that the mental health movement is profoundly secular.

This loss of the soul has had a vast impact on American society. It has led to a culture in which a secular understanding of what it means to be human has emerged as more dominant than the religious view of humans.[49] *Homo psychologicus* has replaced *Homo theologicus.*

As the soul has been whittled away by theology and philosophy, lay people have felt distressed. Psychotherapists have come forward as the dominant "healers" offering to treat these distressed individuals.

In my article "Losing Soul: How and Why Theologians Created the Mental Health Movement," I suggested that the anti-soul climate of twentieth-century theology has created an enormous vacuum in the arena of the self-concepts of lay people. The mental health movement has grown to fill that empty niche.[50]

Secular psychotherapists do not have a coherent and unified theory of the soul. There are more than two hundred different theories of therapy, and each has its own understanding of what constitutes human nature. Secular psychotherapists offer a hungry public an explanation of what each individual life is about. They offer advice about how to live, what one's emotions mean in view of one's childhood in a dysfunctional family, how to relate to a marriage partner, and how to raise one's children. Thus, on an individual, one-by-one basis, therapists are working to provide relief from the famine of information about the human soul. Every important aspect of human life is now considered to be psychological; every important aspect of human life is discussed without ever mentioning God.

This chapter has proposed that the soul has been discarded by theologians and philosophers, that the notion of the soul has been almost abandoned at the end of the twentieth century. Psychotherapists do not offer a replacement for the missing soul. They simply offer to put a bandaid on the wound, to try to help lay people find some relief, one client at a time.

Do Christian counselors offer a theory of the soul to replace that which is missing from theology? Not really. I have profound respect for Christian counselors. But they treat clients one at a time in therapy. Jay Adams, for example, describes a theory of therapy, but not a description of the soul.[51]

Pastoral and biblical counselors have an increasing amount of influence in the religious establishment. However, we should not allow this to obstruct our vision of the painful truth that neither pastoral nor biblical counselors have much influence in the mental health movement; it is, after all, a predominantly secular movement.

A 1987 Gallup Poll suggested that 87 percent of Americans are certain Jesus literally rose from the dead, whereas only 30 percent of mental health experts believe so. That same poll found that 6 percent of Americans are agnostics or atheists, whereas the corresponding figure for mental health experts is 36 percent.[52]

I am a psychiatrist. My psychiatric work is constrained by the guidelines laid down by the American Psychiatric Association: "psychiatrists should maintain respect for their patients' beliefs" and "should not impose their own religious, antireligious, or ideological systems of beliefs on their patients."[53] No matter how you slice the psychiatric pie, it is a secular pie.

Faithful Christians tend to be kind toward their enemies, and therefore they often underestimate the hostility of many psychotherapists toward faith, a hostility hidden behind the therapist's silence. Consider what psychologist Dr. Albert Ellis has written:

> Devout, orthodox, or dogmatic religion (or what might be called religiosity) is significantly correlated with emotional disturbance. . . . The devoutly religious person tends to be inflexible, closed, intolerant, and unchanging. Religiosity, therefore, is in many respects equivalent to irrational thinking and emotional disturbance. . . . The elegant therapeutic solution to emotional problems is to be quite unreligious. . . . The less religious they [patients] are, the more emotionally healthy they will be.[54]

A leading psychiatrist, Dr. David Larson, claims that Ellis has stated what most psychiatrists think but are afraid to say.[55]

If you want to know how ice water feels, talk to seminary professors about the soul. If you want to know how warm water feels, talk to medical school professors about the same subject. We live in odd times: it is physicians such as Dr. David Schiedermayer, not New Testament scholars, who are publishing books on the soul today.[56]

Many religious people today emphasize how psychotherapists are increasingly open to considering the spiritual beliefs of their clients. To some extent, this is true. For example, courses on spiritual beliefs are now offered in some psychiatric training programs, according to *Psychiatric News*.[57] However, this does not change the fundamental point that human nature is predominantly viewed from a secular vantage point in our day. God, if acknowledged at all, is viewed as peripheral, of marginal importance to human nature. Christ is not considered to be the psychological cornerstone. The central human is understood as secular, with the possibility that the person might adorn himself or herself with some abstract "beliefs" in the same way one might wear an earring.

I don't think that secular psychotherapists are capable of giving the soul its proper place in their work; if they did, they would have to acknowledge that one needs to know the Bible to treat the soul. Actually, if therapists were to acknowledge that the soul is the focus of their work, they would soon recognize that the proper training for such psychotherapy is in seminary (assuming that seminaries will change to make room for the soul). Furthermore, controlled clinical trials have shown that group therapy is just as effective as individual psychotherapy. Therefore, why not treat the soul in groups that have God as their focus? The next step in this process would be to say that we should call our psychotherapy groups "churches" or "Bible study."

The question "Who am I?" was a religious question a century ago. It was answered by means of prayer, confession, Bible reading, and worship. Today that question is considered to be a psychological question. It is answered by means of psychotherapy, reading a self-help book written by a therapist, or contemplating one's life within secular assumptions.

This chapter has been a broad-brush sketch of the history of the rejection of the soul by Protestant and Catholic theologians and secular philosophers during the twentieth century. This vacuum contributed to the spectacular growth of the secular mental health movement since 1958. During the twenty-five years I have been involved in the mental health movement, every ten years the number of therapists in North America has doubled. People who have worked under my supervision, who have had neither doctorates nor master's degrees, have left the hospital to go hang out shingles and offer psychotherapy to the public.

The path to life and salvation cannot be obtained by the mental health teachings of self-fulfillment, autonomy, and maximization of one's individual potential as the highest goals of human life. Thus it is both inevitable and tragic that the secular mental health movement leads its clients down a dead-end road.

A Case History

Although, as I have discussed, the soul has been discredited in the twentieth century, the story of Bill Wilson makes it clear that

God has not been asleep.[58] Bill Wilson was an atheist and a chronic alcoholic in the days prior to Alcoholics Anonymous. He worked as a lawyer on Wall Street until he got fired because of his alcohol binges and blackouts. Eventually he was crippled by alcohol, unable to work because his brain was pickled. There were whole years he couldn't clearly remember because of alcoholic amnesia. He was supported by his wife, Lois. She worked, and they lived in the home of her parents. He felt humiliated, ashamed of himself. He felt, correctly, that he had failed at life. For these reasons, he tried to drown his troubles in alcohol.

Another alcoholic, Ebby Thacher, a drunkard more notorious and outrageous than Bill, was going to come over for a visit. Bill was delighted, and set out two glasses on the table, along with a bottle of his best whiskey. When Ebby showed up he stunned Bill by saying that he didn't want a drink. He was now sober. Bill asked how this had happened. Ebby said that he had been defeated by alcohol. He had joined a religious group called the Oxford Group in the Episcopal church, and this enabled him to give up drinking. Bill was indignant that his friend refused to drink with him, and he was offended by religion, but he was also intrigued.

Bill thought that his fate was either death or brain damage from alcohol. He had a few drinks the next Sunday, and wandered into Calvary Episcopal Church on Fourth Avenue in Manhattan, where he listened skeptically to the Oxford Group. At first he was totally resistant and continued drinking. But on his next visit to Towns Hospital for drying out, he became aware how desperate he felt because of his inability to stop drinking.

Bill was alone in his hospital room. He cried out in despair, like a crippled animal, asking if there was a God. He then had a religious experience. He became aware of light filling the room and felt a sense of ecstasy. He said later that it was like standing on a mountaintop and feeling a strong, clear wind blow against him and around him and through him. Bill felt as if he had stepped into another world of consciousness. He had a sense of God's presence. He had a sense of being complete, satisfied, embraced. He became filled with a peace unlike anything he had ever known before.

After this experience, Bill became terrified that he might be losing his mind. His physician, a Dr. Silkworth, reassured him that this had been a valuable experience, representing some sort of tremendous psychological upheaval. Dr. Silkworth told him to trust the experience, even though Silkworth himself was an atheist.

Bill Wilson never had another drink, and he went on to found Alcoholics Anonymous.[59]

3

THE TRIUMPH OF
THE THERAPEUTIC

In 1966 Philip Rieff published *The Triumph of the Therapeutic: Uses of Faith after Freud*. His thesis was that Christianity was dying as a system for organizing society, and was being replaced by Freudian psychoanalysis, which offered individualism with no attempt to organize individuals into any common purpose. "Religious man was born to be saved; psychological man is born to be pleased," Rieff said.[1] Rieff's book was written eight years after Oscar Cullmann put the final nail in the coffin of the immortal soul among New Testament scholars.

Although psychoanalysis has largely died out since Rieff wrote, psychotherapy is offered everywhere—to those who can afford it. Secular television and secular magazines offer the psychological interpretation of what it means to be human, how to seek happiness, and how to deal with other people. God, ethics, morals are rarely mentioned; self-denial and self-sacrifice are never mentioned. Picking up your cross daily to follow Christ in humility is frowned upon as "martyrdom," which is the worst sin in the eyes of most psychotherapists I know.

Rieff suggested that in order to have a culture, it is necessary to have faith and symbols that convince individuals to curtail their self-interest, frustrate some of their lusts, and make sacrifices for the common good. In previous centuries, many Americans had an ideal in whose footsteps they would seek to walk: Jesus. Today, however, American culture encourages each individual to pursue her or his individual interests, to seek fulfillment, pleasure, and that elusive commodity: happiness. A culture in which each individual is seeking his or her own interest and no one is called to make sacrifices for the greater good is no culture at all. It is a civilization unraveling like a bad sweater into individual threads. Because of the disintegration of communal values, individuals are in pain. They get into psychotherapy to become virtuosos on themselves. Yet, when all have become well informed about their individual quirks, their dysfunctional family of origin, how childhood abuse left them damaged, psychotherapy does not inspire the individual to pursue community values (such as running for the school board).

Hundreds of patients have told me that while undergoing psychotherapy, they concluded that they had a "bad marriage," which was impairing their ability to achieve their personal potential. With their therapists' blessing, these patients had gotten divorced, without bothering to have second thoughts about Christ's objection to divorce and without worrying much about the damaging impact that divorce has on children.[2] I have seen what happens to these children who then grow up and come to me thirty years later, still in agony about their parents' divorce, or their father's unwillingness to remain involved with them after the divorce.[3]

I have come to have the cynical view that the secular mental health movement is often like a Mafia-owned construction company I heard about. The company used overweight trucks that caused deterioration of the road surfaces, thereby generating more contracts for the company to repair the roads. One almost suspects that secular psychotherapists encourage divorce—however damaging to children and weak spouses—thereby increasing the need for future psychotherapy.

As a psychiatrist, I see the fallout of divorce. My experience is that divorce is fair to the strong spouse and unfair to the weak and powerless one. Is it any wonder that Jesus was against it?

I am not at all sure it is good for those in the mental health movement to be the primary authorities on what it means to be human in North America. Have North Americans really been feeling better because of this abundant supply of psychotherapy? Research reported in the *Journal of the American Medical Association* shows that during the twentieth century every generation is afflicted with three times as much major depression as the preceding generation.[4] Depression has grown to near-epidemic proportions during this century in which so many psychotherapists have been trying to relieve depression.

Many people consult me for relief of the symptoms of anxiety and stress. On initial evaluation I discover that they have difficult job situations, some with tyrannical bosses, some with threatened layoffs, some with increased demands for productivity. They have come to hate their jobs, and they tell me they are "stressed out." Some of these patients do not suffer from major depression or any other major-league psychiatric disorder. I listen sympathetically, unsure of what I can do to help, because their problems have to do with work. Why they have come to see me is unclear at first.

At the end of the first or second interview, the patients hand me a form for sick leave or disability. Their view is that they have a diagnosis of "stressed out," which has caused them to be disabled, so that they should be excused from work for sick leave and/or go on disability payments. I object that this is not my view. While I am sympathetic that they have job difficulties, I do not see them as sick or disabled. They are all very polite, explaining to me how wrong I am. They are, they repeat, "stressed out." My job as their doctor, they say, is to fill out the disability form or sick leave form. They are astounded that I disagree with this viewpoint.

These dozens of patients appear to think that being "stressed out" is a psychiatric condition that is the opposite of what they think of as "mental health." If you are suffering from "stress," the remedy is to "take good care of yourself" by staying home from work, avoiding responsibilities, and reminding yourself that you are a fabulous person. In this manner, either you are restored to "mental health" or you become permanently disabled.

Dr. Paul Vitz, a psychologist, echoes the same theme as Rieff in his book titled *Psychology as Religion: The Cult of Self Worship*.[5] He claims that psychotherapy has begun to function the way that religion used to function—as an organizing principle of society. Instead of worshiping God, we now worship the self (i.e., we worship and study ourselves). Instead of seeking the salvation of our souls, we seek self-esteem as the highest value. "Self-esteem," Vitz writes, "is based on the very American notion that each of us is responsible for our own happiness."[6]

In North American culture, health and self-esteem are thought to be closely linked, each promoting the other. Vitz says, "Countless Christians worry more about losing their self-esteem than about losing their souls."[7] What is necessary for the health of the soul? Christ said, "Blessed are the meek" (Matt. 5:5) and repeatedly advocated self-sacrifice. To find a healthy soul one must be humble enough to turn to God as the center and origin of value. Vitality comes from God, and does not spring up from inside ourselves—unless we have first incorporated Christ into our lives.

Why would it make sense to live as a servant of Christ? It is because we have been instructed not to worry about ourselves. If we worry about God and God's dominion, God will preserve and nourish our souls. It is like a loving marriage in which the adoring partners lose their self-interest in the union. The secular world tells us to "take care of yourself." The Bible tells us, "forget yourself, and take care of God's agenda."

The unraveling of our culture has been described by Krister Stendahl:

When you are brought up in a bourgeois-Christian, noblesse-oblige society such as I was brought up in in Sweden, you are taught not to expect to be happy. The lower classes might strive to be happy. But a sophisticated person would be looked down upon if their goal in life were to be happy. The goal of life is to serve God, and to take care of one's obligations to others. The word "prestige" can be used only with a negative connotation in the Swedish language. If one is concerned with one's prestige, if one cares what other people think, that is considered a negative attitude. In the society I was brought up in, one is supposed to do what one thinks is right, and let the chips fall where they may, without caring whether other people like you or don't like you. That is how much the Lutheran Church had an influence over the culture. Hypocrisy is the ultimate sin.

But nowadays the culture is different. Now the mental health movement has such a vast influence, especially in the United States, but also in Sweden. Now everyone is out to be happy. What is true and what is right counts for nothing. All that counts is whether the person is going to get re-elected.[8]

Being devoted to the idolatry of self-esteem, as Vitz suggests, North Americans are turning away from corporate or community values such as democracy and sacrificing for one's neighbor. Rather than asking what they can do for God, people are asking what God can do for them. The army used to be able to recruit by saying, "Uncle Sam needs you." But today the army posters say, "Be all that you can be." In the pursuit of the individual goal of self-fulfillment, service to the democracy no longer inspires. Community responsibilities and values are considered to be oppressive.

THE CHURCH'S RESPONSE

Because the mental health movement is more dominant than Christianity in American secular culture, particularly in regard to how we view ourselves, it sets the agenda for how to understand the problems of our day. The problems, therefore, are known as depression, anxiety, and attention deficit—not as human arrogance or sin.

When human problems are defined as depression, anxiety, and attention deficit, the church doesn't have adequate answers and offers only second-rate solutions. Why? Because that list of problems reflects the mental health agenda. However, if the basic human problem were defined as arrogance, and the fact that it is pervasive throughout society (even mental health experts suffer from it), it would be clear that there is no solution but Christ.

There are two nonnegotiable points, however. The first is that theologians can never expect to win a single debate with mental health experts until theologians endorse the soul. If there were some sort of miraculous change of heart, such that Bible scholars wanted to affirm the soul, it would be easy to win such debates by using the argument that psychotherapists treat the soul but do so inadequately.

The second nonnegotiable point is that we must use the despised four-letter word. Sometimes theologians may say "spirit/soul," but then omit the latter term in favor of the former.[9] We cannot get out of the mess we are in by continuing the same bad habits that got us here in the first place.

Of course, the mental health movement is not solely responsible for the secular view of humanity. But psychotherapists are, to a large degree, the mouthpiece of contemporary culture. If you want to know why the purpose and goal of life is (allegedly) self-fulfillment, ask a psychotherapist. This is the gospel found in popular magazines such as *Self, Redbook, Cosmopolitan,* and *McCall's,* as well as dozens of television shows. It is what our culture is teaching the next generation, yet we are shocked when our kids aspire to instant gratification.

Is Christianity Oppressive?

In the American Academy of Religion/Society of Biblical Literature, the largest academic organization of its kind in the world, I have heard many scholars define Christian-based culture as colonial and imperialist, a system against which each individual needs to struggle to define his or her value. Individuals are encouraged to assert the supremacy of their own individualism. Some say the Bible no longer has a coherent meaning; it has no special advantage over Buddhist texts, or the sacred writings of other Eastern religions. Is Christianity oppressive? Does it seek to enslave us?

The notion of Christianity as oppressive sounds vaguely democratic. It sounds vaguely consistent with the value Christ placed on each individual soul. Yet such attitudes are often hostile to authentic Christian faith. They are hostile because they encourage atomistic individualism, and they seek to subvert the requirement that we make sacrifices for God and for our neighbor. Such attitudes encourage self-service at the price of service to others.

The disintegration of community is not solely attributable to the secular mental health movement. There are indeed many other causes.[10] However, it is the mental health movement that preaches a gospel that is intrinsically self-centered, not community-centered, not God-centered. Self-esteem is an idol inside the secular mental health movement. It promotes a culture of self-fulfillment. The emphasis of mental health is on the feelings and lifestyle of the individual, isolated from the social context, removed from the moral fabric within which we live.

Rieff pointed out how American culture was breaking down, from a coherent community organized by shared Christian values to a nation of individuals, each interested in his or her own pleasure and happiness. This atomization of society has many causes. But central to the process, I claim, has been the discrediting of the soul.

Secular psychotherapists seek to help individuals achieve their potential and find relief from oppression. But what is the source of this oppression? Culture is considered oppressive. The Ten Commandments and Christ's expectations of us are sometimes experienced as guilt-inducing. The traditional culture of North America has sometimes been viewed as colonial by women and minority groups. I take the problem of oppression seriously. I was involved in the civil rights movement, was a follower of Dr. Martin Luther King Jr. in Mississippi in 1965, and had an interracial marriage. Further, for a decade I have run the program for battered women at Waterbury Hospital, and another program designed to introduce abusive men to the benefits of civilized behavior (an uphill battle). I do not simply shrug off complaints about oppression.

Nevertheless, there is another side to this phenomenon. The mental health movement has turned us into a nation of victims. If we aren't victimized by abusive parents or spouses, we are victims of cognitive impairment, attention deficit, economic plight, guilt- inducing religion, or subtle discrimination against people exactly like us. It is rare for secular psychotherapists to speak of religion without the modifier "guilt-inducing." Vitz contends that Americans are a pitiful lot, in which the richer you are, the more psychotherapy you have had, and the more you think of yourself as a victim of everything other than your own self-centered narcissism.

It is within this mental health culture that I work. When theologians in the American Academy of Religion speak of Christian culture as colonial, I hear this as another example of the view that we are all shackled victims.

In my own life I have had my share of hardship and tragedy. My father taught me as a young child that the world was about to end in World War III, that we would be vaporized by Russian nuclear bombs, and that there was no hope in life (he was an atheist). Both my first wife and my first son died far too young. Yet these experiences have left me convinced that Christianity is liberating, not oppressive. I view the Ten Commandments as helpful guidelines that allow me to live productively, not as shackles.

The idea that our souls are healthy only when we live within certain boundaries is not popular today. The biblical view that some actions are wrong is rejected as guilt-inducing. But recall this passage from Deuteronomy:

See, I have set before you today life and prosperity, death and adversity. If you obey the commandments of the Lord your God that I am commanding you today, by loving the Lord your God, walking in his ways, and observing his commandments, decrees and ordinances, then you shall live and become numerous, and the Lord your God will bless you in the land that you are entering to possess. But if your heart turns away and you do not hear, but are led astray to bow down to other gods and serve them, I declare to you today that you shall perish. (Deut. 30:15–18)

Repentance is the rhythm of life for a Christian.[11] We constantly stray. In confession and repentance we admit our failures and ask God for the strength to turn our lives around. Slowly the barbarian in us is being Christianized. But secular psychiatry rejects confession and repentance as guilt-inducing, unhealthy, and nontherapeutic.

It was a psychiatrist, Dr. Karl Menninger, who wrote a book titled *What Ever Happened to Sin?*[12] Why do we live in a culture in which psychiatrists, not theologians, ask questions like that? I have pondered Menninger's question for decades. Christian lay people have talked to me about it when I have spoken about the soul at churches. They ask, "Why is there no sin any more? Why is it all 'lifestyle issues'? Aren't some things just plain wrong? Why are there no sermons about sin?"

I think I know the answer. Sin means rebellion against God, insurrection. It means living as if God were unimportant. I believe that the word "sin" has been discredited because sin itself has become the preferred way of life.

What is left when individuals have absorbed enough "therapeutic" medicine from the popular media, and from the army of therapists who have shingles hung on every street corner? What is the net result when everyone has found relief from "oppression" and "guilt-inducing religion"? We are left with a nation of selfish individuals, each preoccupied with his or her own needs, unwilling to make sacrifices for the sake of their families, neighbors, neighborhoods, and communities. Narcissism abounds.

This is the state of self-centered living that the apostle Paul would have defined as "sin." It is what Christ called the wide gate and broad road that leads to destruction. The word "destruction" does not simply refer to what happens after death. It refers first to what is happening in America before our very eyes: destruction of the common good, of the willingness to be taxed or to make sacrifices of time and energy for the sake of our democracy, of the willingness to serve one's country, of values such as the need for common decency with respect to taking care of one's children. North American culture is being pulverized into hundreds of millions of atomic particles, each of which consists of a single individual seeking to be "healthy" by casting off the "oppression" of Christian culture.

Central to this process of destruction has been the triumph of the therapeutic: the loss of faith after Freud, as Rieff said. And central to the triumph of the therapeutic has been the loss of the soul from Christianity.

THERAPISTS *DO* TREAT THE SOUL

Where is the soul today? To whom do Americans turn as experts? I claim that secular psychotherapists are the primary experts.

Sigmund Freud said that his entire life work had been focused on the soul. This, however, is not evident when one reads Freud in English, because James Strachey eliminated the word "soul" when translating the *Standard Edition of the Complete Psychological Works of Sigmund Freud*.[13] In 1905 Freud wrote:

> Treatment of the psyche means . . . treatment arising from the soul [German: *Seele*], treatment of disturbances of the soul [*seelischer*] or body, with methods which first and immediately concern the soul [*Seelische*] of people.[14]

How did Strachey translate *Seele* here? He translated it as "mind," which is a mistranslation.

There can be no question that Freud thought he was treating the soul. Witness his famous comment to Marie Bonaparte: "The great question . . . which I have not been able to answer, despite my thirty years of research into the feminine soul, is

'What does a woman want?'"[15] Some women might applaud Freud for his sudden insight into his own deficiency.

Psychotherapists today avoid using the word "soul." Yet I claim that secular psychotherapists have more names for the soul than Eskimos have names for snow: I, you, myself, yourself, self, psyche, whole person, mind, heart, consciousness, personality, psychic energy, libido, subjective experience, subjectivity, identity, essence, feelings, emotions, cognitive process, thoughts, inner self, human nature, being, inner being, who I am, who you are—all these are names for the soul. And there are dozens more.

If the soul has become a medical, or a psychotherapy, issue, it is treated on an individual basis, as if the soul could be understood in isolation from God, family, or community. For example, most health insurance plans will pay for psychotherapy only if it is done on an individual basis. They will not pay for marital or family therapy.

SOLUTION TO THE PROBLEM

The beginning of a solution to this problem is easier to find than most Christians imagine: we must correctly understand the origin of the problem. Why has psychotherapy replaced Christianity? To reiterate, the triumph of psychotherapy has occurred because of the loss of the soul from Christianity. In other words, the loss of the soul has left a vacuum in the area of self-concept, which has created a vast market for secular psychotherapy.[16]

The soul is a complex matter. Some Christians are reluctant to discuss the soul because it seems to be so self-centered a subject; it seems to be just the opposite of what we should be talking about in our culture. But the soul cannot be truly understood from a self-centered point of view. Intrinsic to the word "soul" in English is a Godward attitude. God is the cornerstone of the soul.

Another way to state this point is to say that the self is the secularized soul. Whereas it is possible to understand myself from a purely self-centered perspective, it is possible to understand my soul only from a theocentric perspective.

Christians need not fear psychotherapeutic examination of who we are, provided that the therapist plays with a full deck. What do I mean by playing with a full deck? In the many years of psychotherapy that I myself have undergone, every therapist has asked me about my relationship with my earthly parents, and yet none has asked me about my relationship with my heavenly Parent. None of those secular psychotherapists, except Dr. Prelinger, has come close to understanding the central psychological issues in my life.

If you play psychotherapy with a full deck, you must discuss the human soul. To fail to do so is to fail to recognize our human nature, for we have within us God's image and we are animated by God's breath. We have a relationship with God, and we can feel fulfilled only if we acknowledge that relationship through prayer, Bible reading, confession, and worship. We are called to embrace New Testament values such as self-denial and loving our enemies and praying for those who hate us. We have a future after death, involving judgment by Christ, and that future is more decisive in shaping who we are today than is the past that we have experienced in our families of origin. Rather than feeling sorry for ourselves for being victims, we can rejoice because of the future that lies ahead and begin preparing for it. "We have this [future] hope, a sure and steadfast anchor of the soul" (Heb. 6:19).

From a theological perspective, there is no other way to understand what psychotherapists treat than to say that they treat the soul, yet many therapists remain completely ignorant about the soul. They have no training. Many refuse to discuss religion. Only 43 percent of them believe in God. No one in his or her right mind would think of going to a secular psychotherapist for treatment of the soul—yet that is precisely what most people do. We live in bizarre times.

Christians must blow the whistle on this insanity. If we even call attention to it, suddenly that which is commonplace in our society will appear to be absurd. If we begin to speak openly, it will become obvious that the "soul" is more interesting than the secular fragment of the soul called the "self" or "secular person." If people do become interested in their souls, and in the health of their souls, churches will appear to be more relevant treatment centers than psychotherapy offices.

Jesus said repeatedly how to find a healthy soul: deny yourself and take up your cross daily and follow him. Those who seek their life will lose it, and those who lose their life for Christ will find it (Matt. 16:25; Mark 8:35; Luke 9:24, 17:33; John 12:25).

4

THE ALLEGEDLY HOLISTIC, UNIFIED PERSON

NOTHING IS SO ATTRACTIVE, or so misleading, as a holistic view of human nature, one that maintains that we are our bodies.[1] Most contemporary theologians, as I have suggested, contend that humans are embodied souls. God created our bodies as well as our souls, and we should rejoice in and enjoy our physical nature. Sexual pleasures are part of God's blessings. Psychosomatic medicine has demonstrated not only that the state of the mind affects the body, but also that the body affects the mind. Indeed, it is impossible to imagine the mind except as it is grounded in the brain. In every respect it would appear that the wholeness of God's created person is a more convincing characterization of our existence than the antiquated view that we are souls inhabiting bodies.[2]

This view of the monistic, whole person is so appealing that it took me two decades of research on the soul before I began to see its flaws. In order to see these flaws, however, I had to rethink my assumptions about who I am.

In the seventeenth century, the philosopher René Descartes described an alternative view of the soul largely unrelated to the body. Descartes' view of the soul-body relationship is ridiculed today. Scholars today assume that Descartes' proposal is absurd because it implies that the subjective person, the one who thinks and feels and reads this sentence, is located outside the body and communicates with the brain only through a tiny connection in the center of the brain, the pineal gland. The pineal gland is a very small projection in the brain, which we now know produces melatonin, a hormone involved in the timing of puberty.[3] This gland becomes calcified and unused by midlife in many people.

The holistic nature of humans is championed in popular media. Life is about feeling good, aerobic exercise, enjoying the opposite sex, dressing well, and looking attractive. I am in favor of these things also. We see in the popular media the embodiment of God's creatures, who are whole and unified creatures and whose bodies affect and reflect their emotions.

Almost all theologians and biblical scholars agree that the holistic and unified view of human nature is biblical. Why is this misleading? What is wrong with this concept?

We are whole and unified people when we are young, but that view of human nature ignores several issues: aging, chronic illness, severe birth defects, and death. As the body grows old and sick, it becomes more and more difficult to reconcile the discrepancies between human nature and the "embodied soul" vision of human wholeness. Television and popular culture deal with this difficulty in a simple manner: rarely do we see the picture of anyone over the age of forty. The models who have posed for photographs in *Self* magazine all appear to be below the age of twenty-five. The holistic and physical embodiment of humans is an image maintained only by the fiction that everyone is young and healthy, a fiction that popular media perpetuate because it is pleasant and flattering.

Ecclesiastes 12:1–7 provides a description of the relationship of spirit and body. Verse 1 describes young people as untroubled, and therefore tending to forget their Creator. Verses 2–5 describe what it is like to be old and feeble: the old person trembles and stoops over (v. 3); grinder teeth are few; vision is poor (v. 4); awakening before dawn, the person is unable to enjoy the song of the birds because of poor hearing (v. 5); fear prevents one from leaving the house, for the person is too fragile; no sexual desire is stirred. Life is broken, shattered (v. 6): "The dust returns to the earth as it was, and the breath returns to God who gave it" (v. 7). Not coincidentally, this last verse, when the human divides into dust and spirit (body and breath), is the converse of Genesis 2:7, in which God creates Adam out of two parts (also see Job 32:8). The terms "breath" and "spirit" are interchangeable here with what we call "soul."

The misleading quality of the holistic view of human nature is illustrated in Ecclesiastes 12:1–7. Only in a youth-oriented culture that wants to avoid looking at old age, chronic illness, severe birth defects, and death, would one imagine that the holistic and unified picture of human nature corresponds to human experience. Certainly at death this "holistic" unity is sundered, for we are not 100 percent annihilated when the body dies and returns to dust. Nevertheless, the holistic wish for youth is attractive: who among us doesn't wish we were young and healthy again?

Would a contemporary theologian insist on a "holistic and unified view" of human nature when looking at a corpse? Clearly there is a physical body that is no longer identified with the whole person. Even if the soul goes into a "spiritual body" immediately after death (which is not what happens), the existence of a cadaver suggests a dichotomous human nature.

As a physician, I spend my working life among those who are left out of this culture of holism. About 80 percent of a physician's time is spent among those who suffer from chronic illnesses. Those who are tortured by their bodies, who suffer from daily pain, fatigue, nausea, or breathlessness, are less enthusiastic about their bodies than theologians would wish. When popular culture tells us that enjoying our bodies is what life is all about, those who suffer from chronic illnesses often say that their lives have no meaning because they cannot achieve the minimum requirement for being human: to have a healthy, trustworthy, and enjoyable body. Throughout America one hears that one's health is of ultimate importance. To lose one's health is to lose everything. In a culture that emphasizes a holistic and unified concept of the human being, those who are not whole, those with amputations and colostomies, mastectomies and dialysis, feel alienated because "life"—holistically speaking—lies beyond their reach.

A holistic and unified view of human beings provides no self-concept for the vast number of humans who are old or sick. To endorse holism implies age discrimination and devaluation of those with disabilities.

Patients in my hospital often tell me that they feel they are no longer part of the human race because they cannot achieve the minimal requirements of being human: to have an energetic, reliable, and comfortable body. Thus when theologians endorse the embodiment of humans, they are asking sick people to bear the burden of self-contempt.

The apostle Paul had some kind of chronic illness, which he described as a thorn in his flesh, "a messenger from Satan, to torment me" (2 Cor. 12:7). Most people with such illnesses are less than fully enthusiastic about their bodies, an attitude one finds in Paul's letters. He wished he could leave his body and be with God (Phil. 1:23–24). Paul described his body as a jar of clay (2 Cor. 4:7), a temporary tent (5:1–6), a place he would prefer to depart from (5:8). He yearned to have his earthly body transformed into a spiritual one, for the earthly vessel was "perishable," "dishonor[ed]," "weak," and subject to Adam's nature (1 Cor. 15:42–54). He beat his body to make it his slave, the way a disciplined long-distance runner must do (1 Cor. 9:27). The estrangement between Paul and his body was so deep that he could even entertain the possibility that he had taken a journey to heaven without his body. He had no idea whether he had taken the trip "in the body or out of the body" (2 Cor. 12:2–4). Anyone who can even imagine taking a trip to heaven without his or her body cannot be thinking of the holistic spirit-body relationship championed by American popular culture and theologians today.

Paul writes that he is carrying Jesus' death around in his body, no doubt a reference to his chronic illness (2 Cor. 4:10–12). In verse 16 he makes this explicit: "outwardly we are wasting away." His bodily life is an "affliction" (v. 17). And in verse 18 he says that his eyes are fixed on what is unseen: eternal glory. One would have a hard time portraying Paul as comfortable in his earthly body.

Such a reading of Paul might elude those who have not had the experience of taking care of thousands of sick people. Paul's reference to the "thorn in the flesh" sounds remarkably similar to the complaints of the medical patients I see.

I know a famous biblical scholar who has had severe asthma and chronic obstructive pulmonary disease much of his life. These complaints have been treated with Prednisone. Over the years the Prednisone has caused osteoporosis, so that his bones have become thin and fragile. The coughing associated with his repeated bouts of bronchitis has caused fractures of his vertebrae, compressing his spine. The cylindrical vertebral bodies have been crushed, causing him to stoop and, more important, resulting in chronic pain. Sometimes when he coughs, as he does frequently during most winters, he fractures ribs. Respiratory medications and Prednisone have also caused a mental fog. Needless to say, these chronic illnesses—especially the pain and the effects of the narcotics—have become obstacles to his scholarly work.

Like most people with such illnesses, this man adopts a dualistic view of human nature. He takes solace in the words of Paul: "Even though our outer nature is wasting away, our inner nature is being renewed day by day" (2 Cor 4:16). His outer nature—his body—is frail, is at times racked with pain, and is something of a burden; but his inner nature—his soul—is revitalized by the Spirit of God. Such people do not find that the meaning of life comes from being embodied. The body is sometimes a cross that must be carried. For some, it is a source of torture.

My first wife, Pat, who died of diabetes over the course of fifteen years, said that she used to feel like a failure every time she became unconscious and was taken back to the intensive care unit of George Washington University Hospital. There she was placed on a respirator and artificial life supports. It was extremely disruptive to everyone's life. As long as she felt identified with her body, and her body was erratic and untrustworthy, she felt humiliated by her own behavior—the price of self-contempt that sick people pay because of the holistic and unified view of human nature. Eventually Pat decided to withdraw her sense of identity from her body, so that she no longer felt like a failure when she was hospitalized. Rather she felt her body had failed, which is what one might expect after being crippled by a dozen diseases. But she could preserve her sense of dignity because she no longer felt that her body was part of her. Her soul was not limited by her feeble body, with its amputated legs and blinded eyes. She died at age fifty.

Pat was a member of St. Columba's Episcopal Church in Washington, D.C. One day the church decided it wanted to create a homeless shelter in the church basement. Many parishioners were interested in helping out, but no one had the leadership skills or expertise to plan such a project, which would require zoning changes, architects, carpenters, and money. Pat had those skills. From her wheelchair, and eventually from her nursing home bed, Pat pulled together a team of parishioners and formulated a coherent plan for tackling the problems one by one. With Pat's leadership, the team was able to get the zoning variances, hire an architectural consultant, raise the required funds, and complete the construction. From her hospital bed, Pat helped the team figure out rules for the homeless people who used the shelter, and she recruited and trained volunteers to staff it. Although Pat died before the St. Columba's homeless shelter had completed its first successful year of operation, she left behind her a highly successful shelter. I cite this to show that Pat's soul had a power beyond that of her disintegrating body.

Caroline Bynum, in her magnificent book *Resurrection of the Body*, says, "Whereas . . . historians all treat the body as a locus of sexuality, I argue that for most of Western history the body was understood primarily as the locus of biological process."[4] The traditional Christian view that the body is sometimes racked with disease is consistent with my view as a physician-theologian.

Holism and Death

The holistic, unified interpretation of human nature fails even more decisively when it comes to understanding death. Most psychiatrists and secular humanists think of humans as holistic, unified, and indivisible. There is no soul-body dualism. If humans are indivisible, by implication the entire human is destroyed when the body dies. Destroy the brain and you destroy the mind—and therefore the person. The end and terminus of human life is six feet below the grass. There is no survival of the human spirit except in the memories of others.

If there is survival after death, as the Bible implies, then it must take one of the three following forms.

Theory 1: Spiritual Body

The first theory is that the spirit immediately acquires a spiritual or imperishable body, as discussed in 1 Corinthians 15: 50–54. I agree with those Pauline scholars who think that Paul was not speaking of death here, but of the transformation of his earthly body if the end of time were to arrive before he died. Let us assume for the sake of argument, however, that Paul meant that at the moment of death the earthly body perishes and there is immediately a spiritual body. This would imply a spirit-body duality.

Theologians who erroneously believe that the spiritual body theory preserves the sense of humans as being whole and unified are unable to explain one thing: why do humans leave corpses behind? If we are whole and unified, our physical body should depart the earth when our spirit does, perhaps transformed like a grain of seed. If we leave a corpse, then we have molted. The inner person and the outer shell have divided. If there is such a thing as a corpse—and clearly there is—humans are not whole and unified when they die.

There are only a few examples in the Bible of people who were (or will be) so unified with their bodies that they left (or will leave) no corpse behind. Enoch did not die but was taken by God, with his body intact (Gen. 5:24; Heb. 11:5). According to ancient tradition, Moses likewise did not die, but was taken bodily by God (despite Deut. 34:5–6).[5] Korah was swallowed by the earth and went down to Sheol alive (Num. 16:30–33). Elijah went up to heaven in a chariot of fire (2 Kings 2:11). Jesus left a corpse behind for three days, but after that the tomb was empty. And the fifth example is the future Rapture, when "we who are alive, who are left, will be caught up in the clouds together with them to meet the Lord in the air" (1 Thess. 4:17; see also 1 Cor. 15:50–54 and John 14:2–3). (This being said, the example of Jesus reminds us that we don't easily understand what the resurrection body will be like. Jesus was able to eat bread and fish after the resurrection, had wounds Thomas could put his fingers in, and yet could become invisible or pass through locked doors whenever he wanted.)

A theologian named Murray Harris has written about the resurrection body being acquired immediately after death.[6] Although I think Harris is wrong, the point I am making here is that even if Harris were correct, we would still need to endorse a dichotomous view of human nature, because humans leave a corpse behind when they die. The corpse that we see on earth is no longer identical with the whole person. The idea that we are our bodies makes no sense at death. The corpse is "inside time," and the spirit is in eternity.

THEORY 2: INTERMEDIATE STATE

The second theory, which is preferred by most New Testament scholars, including Oscar Cullmann,[7] is that there is an intermediate state of existence between death and resurrection. The intermediate state is usually thought to be bodiless.

Obviously the idea of an intermediate state contradicts the concept that humans are whole, unified, and indivisible. If humans are the holistic creatures that popular culture alleges them to be, how could the soul survive after death? Clearly there is some degree of soul-body dichotomy implied by the intermediate state.

There is strong biblical evidence to support the existence of an intermediate state. Matthew 10:28 speaks of those who kill the body but not the soul, and this is echoed in Luke 12:4–5. At the Transfiguration, Jesus met with Elijah and Moses despite their departure from earth centuries earlier (Matt. 17:3, Mark 9:4, Luke 9:30). Jesus spoke of Abraham, Isaac, and Jacob as living, not dead. The spirit of a dead girl was in an intermediate state of bodylessness, so that when Jesus said, "My child, get up!" the spirit returned to her body and she came back to life (Luke 8:52–55). God said, "Thou fool, this night thy soul shall be required of thee" (Luke 12:20 KJV), meaning that the rich farmer's body would die, but also that his soul would depart and stand judgment.

Both Lazarus and the rich man (named "Dives") die and are immediately transported to their respective rewards: Lazarus to the bosom of Abraham and the rich man to the fires of hell. This happens immediately after death, while the rich man's five brothers are still alive, and implies an intermediate state immediately after death (Luke 16:19–31). Similarly, Jesus promises the thief hanging on the next cross: "Today you will be with me in paradise," implying that some kind of reward occurs immediately after death (Luke 23:43).

The Gospel of John promises that the faithful will have eternal life, because they have crossed over from death to life (John 5:24), will live forever (6:51), will never see death (8:51), and shall never perish (10:28). This makes sense only if there is some kind of intermediate state, one that prevents the faithful from becoming nonexistent after death and prior to resurrection.

When Stephen is stoned to death in Acts 7:59, he cries out, "Lord, receive my spirit." Clearly, this spirit is something very different from his broken and dying body.

Paul describes some sort of immediate transformation from earthly body to a postdeath existence in 1 Corinthians 15:35–54. Probably, by the time he wrote 2 Corinthians 4:16–5:10, Paul had come to realize that he would die before the end of history. In the latter passage, Paul describes the immediate survival of death in an intermediate state, without a period of nonexistence before resurrection. Similarly, in Philippians 1:23–24, Paul yearns to depart from the body to be immediately with Christ. And finally, in Revelation 6:9 and 20:4, we read of the souls of dead martyrs without bodies.

The implication of these passages is that we humans are not holistic and unified creatures, that the spirit/soul survives the demise of the body.[8] (This argument is more fully presented in my article "One's Self-Concept and Biblical Theology."[9])

THEORY 3: ANNIHILATION/RE-CREATION

The third possibility for what occurs at death is that we are totally annihilated, then re-created by God *ex nihilo* at the time of the resurrection. (This somewhat bizarre idea was discussed in chapter 2.) Admittedly, the annihilation/re-creation theory raises insoluble philosophical problems about whether there is continuity of identity between who we are now and who we will become when we are re-created.[10]

As I said in chapter 2, no biblical scholars actually endorse the annihilation/re-creation theory, but most imply that it is true. When biblical scholars and theologians speak of the whole, unified human as allegedly portrayed in Scripture, they imply that when the body dies the whole person must be annihilated—we are, after all, our bodies. Because most New Testament scholars acknowledge that Scripture refers to an afterlife, the only solution to this apparent contradiction is to suppose that resurrection means re-creation *ex nihilo.*

This theory, then, is extremely important. Most lay people reason that if there is no soul then death means total extinction—which suggests that Christianity is a fraud. I have known some faithful Christians who became atheists soon after hearing clergy announce that soul-body dualism is not biblical.

Fourteen years after my son Justin died, he appeared to me in a dream and said, "Don't worry about me, Dad, I'm fine!" After that I stopped worrying about him. And two years after my wife Pat died, I had a conversation with her spirit at her grave. It was a delightful talk; she seemed interested in how my life was going and how our daughter Felicity was faring.

I am reluctant to write such things, for we live in such a skeptical culture that such experiences are likely to be ridiculed. Clearly, I cannot prove that these experiences were "real" and not "imaginary." But I do believe that these two people, my son and my wife, were not simply annihilated when their bodies died. The unified view of human nature simply does not fit my experience.

The holistic interpretation of human nature, which is the basis of the secularization of human nature, is attractive but misleading. It is unfair to those with chronic illnesses, severe birth defects, or old age. Further, it fails to allow for Christian hope at death.

If our bodies and souls come apart *at* death, that tells us something about who we are even *before* death. On any given day I might unexpectedly die. On any given day my body and my soul may be torn asunder. How are we to understand human nature in light of this? Are the two parts of a human truly capable of being distinguished prior to death?

MEDICAL SCIENCES

As noted at the beginning of this chapter, René Descartes proposed that the soul is connected to the brain through the pineal gland. Almost everyone today ridicules Descartes, yet the problem he was wrestling with is still with us today. Only one change has occurred in the geography of the soul: I have suggested that we move the location of the dispute from the pineal gland to the entire cerebral cortex. Augustine said that the soul is not located in space, that it is a different kind of substance than the spatial body.[11] If that were true, then we could say that the soul interacts with the cerebral cortex but is not located there, and that the cerebral cortex is not the "seat of the soul." I think Augustine has a point, because neither meaning nor purpose has spatial dimensions, and the soul is largely composed of meaning and purpose.

If you were to ask neuroscientists today whether the mind has an ability to shape the brain based on the goals, purposes, values, and ethics of the mind, you would be contributing to a centuries-old discussion. This is the modern version of Descartes' idea about the soul and the pineal gland. What we call the "mind" would traditionally have been called the "rational soul."

It is incorrect to believe that neuroscientists have proved that brain chemistry and electrical activity totally determine the mind. In fact, there is considerable interest in the opposite effect. For example, Dr. Robert M. Post at the National Institutes of Health has demonstrated that stress can affect the mind, which in turn causes the expression of genes in the brain, which results in a change in brain chemistry or even the sprouting of new branches from the nerves (dendrites), so that the microarchitecture of the adult brain can be altered by the mind.[12]

Modern science is like a Rorschach ink blot test. Those who start with the assumption that the human being is an indivisible unity manage to find their assumptions consistent with scientific research. Simultaneously, those who start with the assumption that human beings consist of two aspects (mind and brain) manage to find their assumptions consistent with scientific research.[13] As I have indicated, I am in the latter camp.

No one has ever had more direct exposure to the human brain than Dr. Wilder Penfield, the world-famous neurosurgeon from Montreal. Years ago Penfield did something no neurosurgeon today would be allowed to do because of contemporary ethical and legal concerns. When a patient needed brain surgery for epilepsy, Penfield would open an entire half of the person's skull under local anesthesia, with the patient awake and talking. When Penfield stimulated different parts of the patient's brain with an electrical probe, the patient would respond that he or she was having intensely vivid memories. With this electrical probe, Penfield mapped out the geography of different functions of the mind within the brain of his conscious patients. He located the areas that controlled the patient's arms, sensation, speech, and memory.

Penfield studied the entire surface of the cerebral cortex in humans by electrical stimulation, searching for the human soul. What he discovered is that the highest functions of the human mind could not be located by such electrical stimulation. There were no areas that could be identified with decision making or abstract reasoning. Nowhere did Penfield locate gray matter that controlled values or ethics. At the end of a lifetime of such research, Penfield concluded that it was easier to explain human nature on the basis of a mind that is somewhat dependent upon, but also somewhat independent of, the brain than on the basis of a single mind-brain unity:

> I worked as a scientist trying to prove that the brain accounted for the mind, and demonstrating as many brain-mechanisms as possible, hoping to show how the brain did so. . . . In the end, I concluded that there is no good evidence, in spite of new methods . . . that the brain alone can carry out the work that the mind does. I conclude that it is easier to rationalize man's being on the basis of two elements than on the basis of one.[14]

Philosopher Karl Popper's ideas formed the working assumptions of neuroscientists during the twentieth century. Popper, coauthor of *The Self and Its Brain*,[15] concluded that human beings cannot be fully explained on the basis of a unitary mind and brain.

Everyone who ponders the human brain soon stumbles upon the central problem. If the mind (which is one aspect of the soul) can be totally explained on the basis of the chemistry and electrical activity of the brain, then we humans are only complex computers. But anyone who works with computers knows how exceptionally stupid they are. I used to teach computing at the National Institutes of Health, and I found that the greatest stumbling block for students was their enormous overestimation of the computer's intelligence. To state the obvious, computers can do only what they are told to do. Human beings are much more than complex computers.

What is omitted from the computer model of human nature is everything significant about being human. The independent and creative reason and ethical honesty of the scientific researcher are not explained by such a model. The human mind has its own integrity that must somehow affect the brain and yet not be completely controlled by the neurochemical constraints of the brain. If the mind has integrity of its own, if it is able to make meaning, set goals, and find purpose, then the mind is semi-independent of the brain. This is the basis in modern science for claiming that there are two parts to a human, only one of which is physical.

However, we must go further. It is not enough simply to say that the cerebral cortex is the seat of the rational soul. The Bible speaks of the soul as being the life force, the energy of every aspect of a living human being. The soul is not simply rational in the Bible. It includes emotions and bodily appetites, as well as the vitality of life itself.

In the Christian tradition, this biblical idea was translated into the concept of a soul with three parts: rational, sensitive, and vegetative. The rational soul was that faculty consisting of thoughts, such as humans have but animals do not. The sensitive soul was the faculty consisting of sensory awareness of the environment, such as animals have but plants do not. And the vegetative soul was the ability to be alive and to grow from within, which is found in all plants and animals.

Today we would say that the rational soul has its seat in the cerebral cortex; that the sensitive soul has its seat in the sensory nervous system, such as the retinas, the optic nerves, and the visual cortex of the brain; and that the vegetative soul has its seat in the DNA, which controls the growth and physiology of every cell in the body. (Although I use the word "seat," I do not think the soul can be located in space, as noted above. The term "seat" is a metaphor that calls our attention to the executive and command functions of the body, with which the soul appears to interact strongly.)

According to ancient tradition, the three aspects of the soul are all parts of a single and unified human soul. When we speak of the mind, we must be clear that the human soul is not limited to the mind. It interacts with the promoter and enhancer parts of the DNA, which control the physiology, life, and death of every cell in the body.[16] The soul described in the Bible is not just rational, but much more.

There is a solid foundation in modern medical research for claiming that a human is made up of two interactive parts: one that consists of organic molecules, and another that brings those organic molecules alive and gives them purpose. It is not possible to explain human nature on the basis of human chemistry, nor is it possible to explain human nature by ignoring our chemistry. We consist of two parts created by God, each of which is necessary for life on this earth, but only one of which survives death (in the "intermediate state"). However, the Bible indicates that without our bodies we are naked and incomplete. Thus the final human hope involves bodily resurrection.

When scholars argue that the Bible teaches that we are whole and unified, they are paving the road for the secular psychotherapists to take over as experts on what it means to be human. When scholars place so much emphasis on the holistic, unified aspect of human nature, and downplay the dichotomy of body and spirit, they are thinking of Plato as the ultimate enemy. But in my fifty years, I have met only one Christian Platonist. I find it hard to believe that teachers and leaders at seminaries have devoted so much effort to defending Christians against Plato, and so little effort at defending Christians against that vast army of mental health experts who seek to explain and treat everything human without mentioning God.

As a psychiatrist, I live among and work elbow-to-elbow with such therapists. Almost all of them believe that death means annihilation—which, if you are a monist, is only logical.

(A "monist" is someone who believes human beings have only one nature that cannot be split into body and soul. The term comes from the word "monad," meaning a unity.) I think it is problematic that Bible experts have not equipped Christians with an anthropology that will defend our flocks from psychiatric wolves. As I have said earlier, most Bible experts I know are opposed to the soul, although the degree of opposition varies. Not all New Testament scholars are completely hostile. Professor Leander Keck, former dean of Yale Divinity School, and president of the Society of Biblical Literature, once told me: "I kind of like offbeat ideas, such as your idea that we should bring back the soul."[17] Still, a dualistic interpretation of the human being is not particularly popular in the world of professional theology.

5

DEFINING — AND REDEFINING — THE SOUL

G IVEN THE MASSIVE EFFORT by theologians and biblical scholars in the first half of the twentieth century to get rid of the soul, it is no surprise that the word is relatively absent from the vocabulary of most theologians and biblical scholars today. Most prefer the word "spirit," believing that spirit is synonymous with soul. But the absence of soul leaves a vacuum—a true deficit in our theological vocabulary. Although soul and spirit are partially synonymous, they are not fully so. Theological anthropology without the soul is like an automobile with four flat tires.

It would make sense to say that secular psychotherapists treat the soul, because *psyche* is the Greek word for soul (ψυχή—the Greek letter "υ" corresponds to the English letter "y"). But it would make no sense to say that secular psychotherapists treat the spirit. They do not call themselves *pneuma*therapists. Neither they nor the public view psychotherapy as "spiritual" treatment.

Because I am convinced that something is wrong in a country that has such an infestation of psychotherapists and that turns to those therapists for advice about every aspect of human life, I feel an agonizing need to redeem the word "soul."

Let me begin by stating the four conclusions that will emerge by the end of this chapter.

1. *The soul is an "oozy" issue, as the classical scholar Catherine Kroeger said.[1] It is difficult to provide any crisp definition of the term soul without finding that it is oozing through one's fingers just as one grasps it. It is like toothpaste. There are a dozen valid definitions. The term is rich and evocative. One of the primary reasons that the soul finds no home in research journals and academic institutions is that no one can corner it, give it a neat little definition, or study it under a microscope.*

2. *"Soul" and "spirit" are often used as synonyms in the Bible. Both refer to the nonphysical aspect of the person. In the New Testament, something of human nature survives the death of the body. That which survives could be called soul (Matt. 10:28; Luke 12:20; Rev. 6:9, 20:4) or spirit (Luke 8:52–55, 23:46; Acts 7:59) or be referred to as the personal pronoun "I" (Phil. 1:23–24; 2 Pet. 1:13–15). Furthermore, it sometimes happens that the word "soul" is used when one might expect "spirit," and vice versa.*

3. *Although synonymous, soul and spirit have different emphases in function in the Bible (see Table 2). Soul directs our attention more to the earthly and bodily aspects of the nonphysical person. The term could be used to refer to unethical impulses or pagans.[2] Spirit directs our attention to the indwelling of God's Spirit. Spirit is a loftier term than soul. Those who are spiritually dead (Matt. 8:22, Luke 9:60) have no spirit, but they are still souls; they are still breathing.*

4. *Theologians, biblical scholars, and clergy need to be realistic about the limitations placed on them by their work. They work predominantly in churches and seminaries, surrounded by faithful Christians. Even those who teach at secular universities have classes filled primarily with believers. Thus the daily work of theologians is primarily with people for whom the soul and spirit are convergent. It comes as no surprise that theologians have difficulty thinking about the discrepancy between soul and spirit. However, if they worked in the wider world, where the majority of people work, they would not have any question about the divergence of soul and spirit. In my secular hospital, for example, many people are spiritually dead, and yet they are obviously still souls, because they are still breathing.*

Table 2   Comparison of Biblical Soul and Spirit

CHARACTERISTIC	SOUL	SPIRIT
This entity is found both in the air around us and within us.	No	Yes
This entity can occupy many individuals, binding them into a unity.	No	Yes
Many of these entities can occupy one individual person.	No	Yes
This term can refer to an evil entity that can invade the individual.	No	Yes
This term refers to the nonphysical aspect of a Christian.	Yes	Yes
This term can refer to the entire person, including the person's body.	Yes	No
This term can apply to non-Christians.	Yes	No
This term can embrace unethical impulses.	Yes	No
This entity is subject to hunger, thirst, and the appetites.	Yes	No

Having stated the conclusions of this chapter, let me now turn to the reasons upon which they are based.

In the Bible, "spirit" refers primarily to spiritual entities external to the person: one thinks of spirits floating about in the air around us. Some of them are evil; God's Spirit is good. The spirit or spirits can invade and dwell inside a person, and thus we can use the term spirit to refer to the nonphysical aspect of a person. But when we do so, we imply that perhaps the spirit inside may have originated outside. Is the spirit of a Christian the same as the Christian's native personality, or is it the Holy Spirit that has come inside to dwell? This is ambiguous. The more Christianized a person becomes, the more regenerated and sanctified he or she becomes and the more every aspect of his or her life becomes infused with God's Spirit (see John 3:5–8 or Romans 8). In the New Testament, at least, there is no clear distinction between the spirit of Paul or John, say, and the Spirit of God (i.e., in the writings of Paul and John it is often difficult for translators to decide whether *pneuma* should be translated as Spirit with a capital "S" or as spirit with a small "s").

The term soul can also refer to the nonphysical aspect of a person. But it is not external as is the spirit. The soul never exists outside the human body during this life. After death the soul can be outside the body (see Rev. 6:9 or 20:4), but during this life the soul cannot depart from the body; to suggest otherwise is to suggest that the individual has died.

Thus we can say that soul and spirit are synonyms because both refer to the nonphysical aspect of a person, the part that survives the death of the body. At the same time, we must acknowledge that they imply different things. The term soul includes every aspect of a person, such as the person's ethically negative impulses.[3] For example, unlike the spirit, the soul encompasses hatred, lust, and the impulse to rape (2 Sam. 5:8; Song of Sol. 1:7, 3:1–4; Gen. 34:2–3, 8). Only the soul is subject to bodily appetites such as hunger and thirst (Num. 11:6; Ps. 107:5; Prov. 6:30, 25:25, 27:7 KJV). Only the soul is temptable (1 Pet. 2:11), dies if it sins (Ezek. 18:4 KJV), can be forfeited (Mark 8:36), and is savable (James 1:21).

The terms soul and spirit are clearly not synonymous in Paul's letters. Two out of the three biblical verses that distinguish between soul and spirit were written by Paul (1 Cor. 15:45, 1 Thess. 5:23, Heb. 4:12). In 1 Corinthians 15:42–49, Paul constructs a series of parallels between the first Adam as a "soul" (KJV or ASV) and the last Adam (Christ) as a "spirit" (v. 45). The parallelism implies that the soul is "perishable," "dishonored," "weak," "of the dust of the earth" (v. 47), "earthly" (vv. 48–49) and "natural" or "soulish" (vv. 45–46). Paul uses the Greek word *psychikos* the way the word was used elsewhere in the first century, to refer to the "soulish," earthly, or natural quality of humans.[4] "Soulish" and "spiritual" individuals are contrasted by Paul in 1 Corinthians 2:14 and 15:45–46.

Soul was not one of Paul's favorite anthropological terms;

he used the word to refer to the natural condition of humans before they were saved. It referred either to life (Rom. 11:3, 16:4; Phil. 2:30) or to the self (2 Cor. 1:23, 12:15; 1 Thess. 2:8), but it did not imply anything spiritual. When theologians assert that soul and spirit are completely synonymous, they should recall Paul's letters.

The most obvious discrepancy between soul and spirit is found in biblical references to census taking. These numerous references concern the counting of souls, not spirits (Gen. 12:5, 46:15, 18, 22, 25–27; Exod. 1:5, 12:4; Acts 2:41, 7:14, 27:37). There is always one soul per person, no more and no less.

This is not true, of course, in regard to spirits. The New Testament makes clear that one person can be occupied by several evil spirits (Luke 8:2, 30–33; Mark 5:9-13; 1 Cor. 12:10; 1 John 4:1, 6). In the case of Legion, a single man was occupied by ten thousand evil spirits, or demons. Alternatively, there can be one spirit of unity shared by many people (Rom. 15:5, 1 Cor. 12:4, Phil. 1:27).

The soul is the life force of a unique individual. There is always one soul per person, which never departs until that person dies. The term soul refers to that which is idiosyncratic and natural to that person, regardless of whether the person is saved or unsaved.

Spirit is a term that considerably overlaps the term soul. There is an oozy and indistinct difference between the terms— a difference in emphasis. Spirit refers more to the spiritual aspects of a person, such as the occupation of that person by many evil spirits, or by God's Spirit. My primary definition of the biblical term soul, which I introduced at the beginning of this book, is *the inner or subjective person in the natural state, whether saved or unsaved.*

In the Introduction I pointed out that there is a nuance or elaboration that is needed to clarify this first definition. From an ontological viewpoint the soul and spirit are identical, both referring to the inner or subjective person, that which survives between death and resurrection. From a functional viewpoint the word "soul" emphasizes the horizontal and the word "spirit" emphasizes the vertical aspects of that one inner person. Furthermore, when we say "in the natural state," we need to clarify that "natural" means fallen nature as we observe it around us. Prior to the Fall, and after regeneration, we will discover that human nature is more noble than we often find on earth.

When theologians and clergy assert, as they often do, that the term soul is not needed because it is encompassed by the term spirit, what is missing is precisely that which secular psychotherapists treat: the inner person in the natural, earthly state. The reason that the secular mental health movement exists is because it fills the vacuum left by theologians' unwillingness to acknowledge or address the soul. (This is discussed in depth in my article "Losing Soul: How and Why Theologians Created the Mental Health Movement."[5])

If Christians consist of body and spirit, as so many theologians have told me, how would they describe those who are spiritually dead? It would be absurd to describe such people as bodies only—and yet this is the logical conclusion to which one is driven by the deficient anthropology found today in theology.

PURITY OF THE SOUL

Although in the Bible the term soul is somewhat earthly in emphasis, the word has been whitewashed in the Christian tradition. By "whitewashed" I mean that it has taken on more and more spiritual meanings, as if the soul were always pure. It is difficult to imagine how the biblical soul could be so if one thinks of Genesis 34:2–3, 8, in which the soul of Shechem lusted after and raped Dinah, or of 2 Samuel 5:8, in which David's soul hated the Jebusites (KJV). The biblical soul includes what we in the mental health movement would call the personality or the mind or the libido. Sometimes the human mind worships God; sometimes it is given to lust and hatred.

It is easy to understand why the soul has assumed such an image of purity over the centuries. We human beings do not like to admit what depraved creatures we are. In recent years we have witnessed genocide in Bosnia, Croatia, Rwanda, Zaire, Liberia, and Cambodia. The North American continent was settled by Europeans who practiced genocide against Native Americans. Yet we deny such depravity. When Christians have emphasized the purity of the soul, they have given in to the desire to see human nature in this fallen world as noble—far more noble, in fact, than that which the Bible describes.

Philosophers such as Plato and Plotinus also contributed to this concept of a "pure" soul. They identified the soul with the rational thinking of philosophers such as themselves. The soul became a philosophical construct. In this way, the term soul took on a meaning quite far removed from its biblical meaning.

Let me be clear: The soul that is the focus of this book is the biblical soul, not the soul of philosophical circles or even the soul found in the Christian tradition. Because the word soul is mostly dead in our culture today, why not begin to use it in a biblical way?

TEN ASSOCIATED DEFINITIONS

The soul has been described in this chapter as an "oozy" issue, one that is difficult to define with precision. If one attempts to clutch the soul and offer a crisp definition of it, as I have, its meaning begins to trickle between one's fingers.

I have surveyed 248 clergy and theologians—54 Catholic, 57 United Methodist, 72 Episcopal, and 65 members of the conservative Evangelical Theological Society—asking them to define the soul. From those surveys I arrived at eight additional definitions of the term, as well as another two that are unique to the Catholic church.

1. THE SOUL IS THE VITALITY OF LIFE,
AN ENERGY GIVEN BY GOD

When Bible translators systematically removed most occurrences of the word "soul" from twentieth-century translations ("soul" occurs 533 times in the King James Version but only 88 times in the Living Bible), the word they most commonly chose to replace "soul" was "life."[6] This word was chosen because the soul was believed to be the life force, the breath that sustained us. Consider the following (in this and all subsequent biblical extracts in this section italics are mine):

> [Elijah] stretched himself upon the child three times, and cried unto the Lord, and said, O Lord my God, I pray thee, let this child's *soul* come into him again. And the Lord heard the voice of Elijah; and the *soul* of the child came into him again, and he revived. (1 Kings 17:21–22 KJV)

In twentieth-century translations, "soul" was changed to "life" in these verses. Consider further the following passage from the King James Version:

> Thou fool, this night thy *soul* shall be required of thee. (Luke 12:20)

In twentieth-century translations, this passage became

> You fool! This very night your *life* is being demanded of you. (NRSV and New International Version)

> Fool! Tonight you die. (The Living Bible)

All these translations are valid, because the words *nephesh* and *psyche* can mean either life or soul. Actually, there are many other possible ways to translate these Hebrew and Greek words. In the New International Version, 153 different English words are used to translate the Hebrew *nephesh*, and 31 different English words are used to translate the Greek *psyche*.[7]

Even the KJV translators frequently used the word "life," as in this verse:

Therefore I say unto you, Take no thought for your *life*, what ye shall eat, or what ye shall drink; nor yet for your body, what ye shall put on. Is not the *life* more than meat, and the body than raiment? (Matt. 6:25 KJV)

Here it is clear that "life" is a better translation than "soul."

God breathed into a lump of clay to make Adam come alive (Gen. 2:7; see also Job 32:8, Eccles. 12:7). It is possible to think of the visible person as the body, and the invisible or inner person as the soul/spirit. This inner aspect consists of the mind, thoughts, and emotions, but it also consists of the vital energy that makes us animated. For this reason, the early theologians distinguished the rational soul from the vegetative soul, which we would call the mind and physiology, respectively. In the Bible, the vegetative soul was located primarily in our breathing, which made us alive.

2. THE SOUL IS THE WHOLE PERSON, INCLUDING THE BODY AS PART OF THE SOUL

The biblical words for soul often refer to the entire human, by the linguistic twist called synecdoche. For example, as we said before, census takers in the Bible counted the number of souls. Twentieth-century translations replace "soul" with "people" in these verses, which is reasonable.[8] The King James Version says, "Let every soul be subject unto the higher powers" (Rom. 13:1). Here Paul urges each person to accept the authority of earthly governors. The term soul has been translated as "person" in twentieth-century Bibles, because "soul" refers to the whole person, including (by implication) the person's body.

Because the term soul often refers to the whole person, it is often translated as a personal pronoun in twentieth-century versions. For example, the King James Version says:

And fear came upon every soul. (Acts 2:43)

But modern translations read, "fear came on everyone." In the King James Version, God says:

Behold my servant, whom I have chosen; my beloved, in whom my *soul* is well pleased. (Matt. 12:18)

But the New International Version reads, "in whom *I* am well pleased."

Translation reflects an interpretation of the Bible. All these translations are valid, because the Greek word *psyche* could refer to the soul or could be a personal pronoun. One's choice of which term to use reflects a judgment call about what kind of a spin you want to put on the ball. The King James translation emphasizes the sacred nature of each person by calling the person a soul, whereas the twentieth-century style is much more secular. Our current Bibles have been translated by scholars who avoided the word "soul," preferring to use terms such as "person" or personal pronouns.

The point is that the word soul could refer to the whole person in the Bible. By implication, we would have to say that the body could be part of the soul, because the body is part of the person. This is not an idea that has been part of traditional theology, but it is biblical. (A similar use of "soul" is found in English nautical vocabulary. In World War I, ships used Morse code, and the term "S.O.S." meant "Save Our Souls." Here "soul" refers to the whole person. "Save Our Souls" means "Save Our Sailors," but "souls" is much more urgent and poetic than "sailors." Similarly, the children's rhyme says, "Old King Cole was a merry old soul," where "soul" means "person.")

3. THE SOUL IS THE NONPHYSICAL ASPECT OF A PERSON
As noted earlier, our primary definition of the word soul is the inner or subjective person. By implication, this refers to the aspect of a person that is not visible, not physical. You can touch the body, but you cannot physically touch the soul. This nonphysical aspect could be called spirit or soul. If the body is destroyed, the implication is that the nonphysical part of the person is not destroyed. Thus, in Revelation 6:9 and 20:4 we read about the "souls" of saints who have been beheaded.

We psychiatrists call the nonphysical aspect of a person the "mind." But in the Bible this notion includes the life force, the breathing and animation of the body. Indeed, the Latin word for soul was *animus*, because it was believed that every animate (i.e., "moving") body had a soul. We may find this distinction between body and life to be odd, but only because we do not like to dwell on what happens to a person at death, when the body dies but the life force does not.

4. THE SOUL IS ONE'S INDIVIDUAL UNIQUENESS

Although this kind of definition is not specifically mentioned in the Old and New Testaments, it is plausible to suggest that it is at least consistent with the Bible.

As I remarked earlier, each soul is unique to each individual, and can be thought of as the person's unique qualities: their idiosyncrasies and foibles, their warts and personality style. Contrast this with the term "spirit," which appears to be a more generic term, something that can be shared by many people. Thus, what makes a person unique and different from other people is the soul, not the spirit.

5. THE SOUL IS THAT WHICH PROVIDES CONTINUITY BETWEEN THIS WORLD AND THE NEXT

What survives when the body dies? In the Bible it is the soul (Luke 12:20; Rev. 6:9, 20:4) or spirit (Eccles. 12:7, Luke 8:52–55, Acts 7:59). Theologians debate whether what survives is, at first, bodiless ("naked," as Paul says in 2 Cor. 5:3) or has a "spiritual body." My own view is that it is impossible to imagine a soul without some boundary or definition or shape. Just as a radio wave must have a frequency, a soul must have something to define what is, and what is not, the individual person. That "something" is a body or a spiritual body, or, as Thomas Aquinas says, the "form" of the body.

6. THE SOUL IS THE PERSON AS SHE OR HE RELATES TO GOD

Throughout the Bible the person's soul or spirit relates to God. For example, one lifts up one's soul unto God (Ps. 25:1, 143:8), prays to God in bitterness of soul (1 Sam. 1:10, 15; Job 7:11, 27:2;

Ps. 6:3), or turns to God with all one's heart and all one's soul (1 Kings 2:4, 8:48; 2 Kings 23:3, 25; 1 Chron. 22:19; 2 Chron. 6:38, 15:12, 34:31). God restores one's soul (Ps. 23:3). The Law of God is perfect, reviving the soul (Ps. 19:7).

When we speak of the soul as that which relates to God, we tend to think of some inner or mysterious or secret part of ourselves, akin to a spirit inside a concealed chapel. Yet I prefer to think that in this sense the word soul could refer to the whole person. Just as I sin with my whole person, just as I go to work or relate to my wife as a whole person, I similarly relate to God with my whole person.

7. THE SOUL IS THE ESSENCE OF A PERSON

The Bible does not explicitly state that the soul is the essence of a person, but it does reveal how God views us. I often think of my soul as being the person God views me as being. God knows us perfectly (Ps. 103:13–14, 139:1–2; 1 John 3:20). The person God knows me to be is my essence, the real core of who I am, without the lacy curtains of denials and rationalizations.

The idea that the soul is the essence of a person was emphasized by Saint Augustine. It was Augustine, revealing the influence of Plotinus, who first understood the soul as an inner space, a psychological process of autobiographical introspection.[9]

8. THE SOUL IS THE IMAGE OF GOD INSIDE A PERSON

The Bible indicates that we carry the image of God as part of our human makeup (Gen. 1:26–27, 9:6; 1 Cor. 11:7). According to the New Testament, we are progressively becoming like Christ; we are progressively renewed in the image of God (Col. 3:9–10). Theologians who avoid using the term soul frequently use this notion of the image of God instead.[10] As I have indicated, however, I am convinced that the soul is not as noble or as pure as the image of God. The soul can be fallen, which in truth is the natural state of humans in the world in which we live.

84

9. THE SOUL IS THE FORM OF THE BODY

This definition comes from Thomas Aquinas, who adopted it
from Aristotle.[11] Aristotle used the analogy of building a house
to express his interpretation: the soul is the architectural plan,
whereas the body is the lumber. Put another way, the soul is the
active principle, which controls the overall design, vitality, and
growth, whereas the body is the passive principle, or poten-
tiality. The soul is what takes the stuff of sheer matter and
transforms it into a living human being.[12]

Aquinas and Catholic theologians have rejected Platonic
dualism. The soul is not separate from the body, is not a different entity, but is the substantial form of the body. The soul cannot enter the body of a fetus, for without a soul there would be
no fetus; that is, the fetus could not have a form without a soul.
Rather, the soul is created by God, and receives the fetal body
immediately into communion with itself at conception, some
Catholic theologians say. At death the body is lost, but the soul
remains in relation with the body—a mystery we cannot understand. The whole person is restored when the body is resurrected into communion with the soul in heaven.[13]

Whereas Protestant interpretations of the soul derive directly from the Bible, Roman Catholic interpretations often derive from the Bible as understood through the lens of the
scholastic tradition. As a Protestant, I would caution that it is
impossible to think about the soul without making philosophical assumptions. According to Catholic theology there is only
one substance, which consists of the soul as the form, and the
body as the matter shaped by that form. Thus we have only one
nature.

10. THE SOUL IS THE FIRST PRINCIPLE OF LIFE

Thomas Aquinas wrote, "To seek the nature of the soul, we
must lay down first that the soul is defined as the first principle of life in those things which in our judgment live; for we call
living things 'animate,' and those things which have no life,

'inanimate.'"[14] (The Latin word for "animate" is the same as the word for "soul.") He goes on to say that the soul is an incorporeal substance.

Is there a biblical basis for this definition of the soul? Yes. Throughout the Bible the most fundamental concept of the soul is that it is the breath of life that animates an animal. When it departs, the animal dies. The Hebrew word *nephesh* is used to describe both animals and humans. In the human, the *nephesh* consisted of not only the vital energy but also the inner psychological processes, the subjective point of view, the thoughts and emotions and spiritual aspects of the person.

Similarly, Aquinas contends that every living thing has a soul. Plants have a vegetative soul (a physiology). Animals have a soul with both sensitive and vegetative functions (a sensory nervous system and physiology). And human beings have a rational soul with intellectual, sensitive, and vegetative functions (a mind in addition to a sensory nervous system and a physiology). This Thomistic interpretation is consistent with both the Bible and modern medicine.

What does "the first principle of life" mean? Let us compare and contrast Aquinas' idea with the concept of DNA I proposed in chapter 1. DNA is considered by many to be the first principle of life. Without DNA there is no life. It is DNA that shapes and controls the organic molecules from which our body is built. The DNA of a fertilized egg causes the growth of the egg according to the architectural plan embedded in the DNA. Thus the genetic plan determines whether the organism is a tree, a horse, a dinosaur, or a human; it determines the color of one's eyes and whether one's nose is large or small. Research in recent decades indicates that certain aspects of our personality may be genetically influenced. This is what is meant by the first principle of life.

Yet this is a materialistic way of thinking about humans, and differs from Aquinas in two ways. First, Aquinas emphasizes the nonphysical aspect of the soul. To say that everything about humans can be reduced to a biological basis is reductionistic.

Certainly, as I have tried to point out in earlier chapters, biology cannot explain everything. Second, Aquinas contends that the animal soul is different from the human soul—humans have a rational soul that is not shared by our nonhuman counterparts on earth. Only human beings can rebel against God.

Consider what I would be like if you removed my intellect and will. Suppose, for example, I suffered from brain death or profound dementia (Alzheimer's). My body would not look the same. My face would be expressionless, my eyes would be glassy and no longer the windows of my soul. (This is known as "persistent vegetative state.") In this condition the rational soul is gone, and what is left is a vegetative soul. One is known in this condition, of course, as a vegetable.[15]

The soul is the principle of being, according to Catholic theologians. If we distinguish a being from the principle of being, the former is the body and the latter is the soul. The soul is not an entity that exists for its own sake. Rather, it gives direction and orientation to the body. It is the intrinsic source of being. Thus body and soul comprise a single entity.[16]

Cohesiveness of the Concept of the Soul

With so many definitions of the soul, one has the sense of a thousand flowers blooming. Clearly there is a rich diversity of meanings to the word. But is there any cohesiveness, anything that pulls these divergent definitions together into a coherent concept? The answer is yes. The word "soul" refers to human nature vis-à-vis God. There is an intrinsic Godward orientation to the term. I have often said that the most exciting definition of "soul" would be the person God knows me to be.

I love the word soul because it brings us face-to-face with what is missing in much of American culture: the recognition that God is central to one's self-concept, that we cannot begin to understand human nature unless we start with God's relationship with us. Without the word "soul," the road is paved for a completely secular understanding of humans, as if God were irrelevant to our self-image.

SOUL VERSUS SELF

In secular society, the word "soul" has been replaced by the word "self." (Recall Table 1 in the Introduction.) Because the soul is missing from the scene, the self has taken over as the consuming interest of secular culture. Mental health leaders such as Carl Rogers, Abraham Maslow, Rollo May, and Heinz Kohut have promoted the self as the central focus of psychotherapy. Kohut's form of psychotherapy is even named "Self Psychology." When you hear the word "narcissism" today in the mental health movement, it usually implies Kohut's Self Psychology—that is, a comprehensive theory of the soul that never mentions God.[17]

When researchers in the secular mental health movement study humans and their natural tendencies, they discover that the virtues or goals of life are autonomy, self-sufficiency, individuation, differentiation from other people, self-fulfillment, and the maximum achievement of personal potential. These are the inherent tendencies of the self or soul, which Paul described as our "old Adam"—our fallen nature. What makes these virtues sound like vices is that they convey the pre-Copernican view of human psychology in which God and other humans revolve around the self. The central emphasis is on "me." If you are important, it is because you meet or frustrate my needs, not vice versa. If God is relevant, it is because God strengthens my self-esteem or weakens it by making me feel guilty. I am the center of the psychological galaxy, according to the old Adam of original sin. It is our natural tendency to be this way if we are not converted, born again, regenerated, and sanctified.

When a person becomes converted, saved, born again, the Spirit enters and begins the process of transforming the soul. Thus a Christian has two tendencies, often at conflict with one another: One is the soulish tendency to pursue self-interest as the highest goal in life; the other is the spiritual tendency to devote oneself to God and neighbor, even at the risk of self-sacrifice.

Through the process of regeneration and sanctification, the soul is slowly transformed in a Christian, so that it takes on more and more identity with the spirit. Over time the soul and spirit converge, becoming increasingly identical. The convergence of soul and spirit is a process that occurs in the psychological makeup of Christians.[18] It is a process that can be called "sanctification."[19] This process means that the self is invaded and transformed by the Spirit, so that what the self wants is what God wants.

At first it does not seem natural to do what God wants us to do. Atheists and agnostics rebel, feeling that if they were to give in to God they would become subjugated and lose their integrity. But as one is gently transformed by the Spirit working quietly inside like yeast, leavening the entire loaf (Matt. 13:33, Luke 13:21), one slowly begins to understand that self-interest is identical with God's interest.

This is why psychotherapy can be helpful to Christians. For those who are saved, the self and the spirit are increasingly convergent. Thus the ultimate goal of psychotherapy is different for Christians than for others. The goal is not autonomy, self-sufficiency, and independence of God. The goal, rather, is to rid ourselves of the tendency to lie to ourselves. Psychotherapy can further this process. Even when the therapist is an atheist, such therapy can serve the purpose of regeneration and sanctification, because it brings the lies and selfishness of our old Adam nature into focus so that we can see the enemy within.[20]

6

THE SOUL AS SOURCE OF HUMOR AND WIT

THE EMOTIONAL CHALLENGE IN medical training is understanding one's own mortality. The democracy of death does not recognize physicians to be made of a different stuff than that common mortal fabric that disintegrates from ten thousand diseases. Not even a king is immune: as Hamlet said, "A man may fish with the worm that hath eat of a king, and eat of the fish that hath fed on that worm" (*Hamlet*, IV, iii, 29).

It is not just the dissection of a cadaver, but the entire confrontation with the overwhelming evidence of morbidity and mortality, that makes medical school so anxiety-provoking. Most of us contracted a series of those famous maladies called "medical student diseases"—the acute onset of symptoms of a heart attack when studying the cardiovascular system, ulcerative colitis symptoms when studying the colon, joint pain when studying arthritis, and psychosis when studying psychiatry. A friend of mine awakened during his studies of neurology with the certainty that during the night he had had a stroke that had obliterated both sides of his brain, so that he was completely unable to move a single muscle on either side of his body. He was terrified. Then he realized that he had contracted yet another form of "medical student disease." Upon arriving at the correct diagnosis, he got out of bed, shaved, and went back to medical school, relieved that the stroke had vanished like a dream. During medical school I made a half-dozen frightened appointments with my physician, expecting to be told that I had cancer or was going blind. Every time the exam was normal.

It was during internship, working an average of 110 hours a week, that my identity as an ordinary human was thrown into the fiery furnace and forged into a new identity as a physician. During internship one is faced with relentless tragedies in which, on average, the forces of death and disease are winning the battle against the miracles of modern medicine. An infant is born with a Wilm's tumor and proceeds to die of the cancer with which it was born. Colostomies are surgically constructed in dignified adults who do not deserve such indignities. It is not the horrors one must face that change a physician's identity, but the need to remain calm and thoughtful in the face of horror. Life-and-death decisions must be made by a physician, and therefore the physician cannot afford to turn away, to vomit, to faint, to become numb and stop thinking, or to be overwhelmed by the thought, "This could happen to me."

Two weeks after graduating from medical school, I was working as an intern in a cardiac care unit and was the only physician there in the middle of the night. At 2 A.M., a nurse phoned to say that I must come at once. I stumbled out of bed, ran down the halls, and entered a dark room in which there were two patients and two nurses. The nurses were looking anxiously at me. Beside them was an old man in bed, hooked to a cardiac monitor, which showed that the patient's heart rate was getting slower and slower. I had only two thoughts: It looks like he has about one more minute to live, and I wonder if this is really happening, or whether I am dreaming. I could think of nothing else— no medical information, no knowledge of cardiac disease.

Instinctively, I knew that coronary care nurses know what to do in such situations but are prohibited by protocol from saying so. I said, "Someone tell me what it is I want."

A nurse said, "I think you want atropine, doctor."

"That's right," I replied. "I do want atropine. And someone tell me how much atropine I want."

"I think you want about 1 cc, I.V. push, doctor," the nurse said.

"Thank you," I said. "Please give it."

The nurse drew up 1 cc of atropine into a syringe, pushed it into the man's intravenous tube, and within a few seconds the cardiac monitor showed that his heart rate had returned to normal. Everyone smiled and looked at me as if I were a genius.

What is the moral of this story? The moral is that when human life or death depends on what one says, a physician must act in a responsible way, whether one likes it or not. Neither sleeplessness nor feelings of horror can be tolerated if a patient might die because one allows oneself to feel overwhelmed.

Within the fiery furnace of internship I learned the trick most physicians use to fend off anxiety about their own mortality. That trick is to tell oneself a lie—that one is immortal. Scratch the surface of almost any physician and you will discover a covert and unstated assumption that the physician is not made of the same fragile flesh as the rest of humanity, but is, like the Greek gods, immortal. Thus physicians are notorious for taking risks, such as flying airplanes in ways that others would consider dangerous, or hang gliding or skydiving or whitewater rafting. It has been said that the difference between God and a physician is that God knows that God is not a doctor.

You may think it arrogant for doctors to entertain such an absurd self-image. But few readers would be able to work as physicians for longer than a single day, because of the appalling emotions that are stirred up as one watches every person eventually succumb to disease and death.

It is moral and ethical for us as physicians to believe in our own immortality, because it is the only way we are able to fulfill the responsibility to our patients of remaining compassionate and involved with people who are being crucified by disease. We are therefore able to think rationally under conditions in which others would become numb. Seasoned soldiers probably are able to continue to function during a firefight because they tell themselves that they are immortal, unlike the soldiers beside them who have just been blown to bits.

The rudest and most unacceptable behavior among physicians is for a colleague to become ill or die. It is rude because it makes the medical community aware of what we know but don't want to admit to ourselves—namely, that our ability to work is based on a lie. When a doctor is hospitalized, other doctors whisper to one another in hushed tones, as if it were a scandal. A physician who becomes disabled by disease has, by definition, crossed over from the realm of the gods to the realm of mere mortals.

Many people may believe that it would be rewarding to be a physician because they see doctors curing disease on television, but what doctors do on television has little relationship to reality. It is true that doctors cure some diseases, but this is only a small part of what we do. At least 80 percent of a physician's time and energy is spent dealing with chronic diseases for which there are no cures. Perhaps the majority of people who go to a doctor are helped, but it is the treatment failures who come back again and again, so that from where we stand we are far more aware of the irreversible illnesses, which consume 80 percent of the health care resources, than of the reversible illnesses, which consume only 20 percent.

What is human nature? Is the lie of immortality a truth, and the truth of mortality a lie? Herein lies a paradox that offers the potential for considerable mirth.

Physicians and clergy are, in a peculiar way, similar. Both are exposed to what appears to be commonplace theodicy. ("Theodicy" is a theological word for unfair suffering, or suffering that appears to be unfair.) The public, overwhelmed by fear of their own morbidity and mortality, turn to both physicians and clergy for solace. Practitioners of both professions use a similar concept of immortality to fend off the anxiety that might arise if one were to think that one were going to die, as did King Claudius and Hamlet.

As an ordained minister, I regularly receive letters from the bishop announcing the death of one minister or another. The fact that I also am mortal is implicit. Yet such an announcement is not anxiety-provoking because the unstated assumption is that our colleague will somehow survive death, because death is a doorway to something better and is a relief from suffering. As Shakespeare said, through his character the Bishop of Carlisle, when the Duke of Norfolk died, "And there at Venice gave his body to that pleasant country's earth, and his pure soul unto his captain Christ, under whose colors he had fought so long" (*King Richard II*, IV, i, 97).

As I pointed out at the outset of this book, being both a physician and a clergyman makes me a Dr. Jekyll and a Rev. Hyde. As Dr. Jekyll I have been trained to adopt the lie of immortality, as if I will never get sick and die like everyone else. As Rev. Hyde, I have been trained to adopt the assumption that I will transcend death, which allows me to calmly contemplate the inevitability of my own sickness and death. The basic anxiety of a pastor is not that he or she must die, but that there will be judgment after death. Some kind of immortality is implied by both professional roles.

But there are two different varieties of immortality. Dr. Jekyll avoids thinking about it because it might be a lie. Rev. Hyde assumes it to be true, but avoids thinking about it because biblical scholars and theologians dodge the question of the immortality of the soul, saying it is a Greek idea that the biblical theology movement has branded as "unbiblical." The allegedly unbiblical nature of the soul is a chronic illness from which Christendom has not recovered.

Here, then, is an absurdity—that somehow immortality allows us to function—and yet we are hogtied and unable to discuss that paradox which is the truth, and that truth which is a paradox.

THE DEATH OF IMMORTALITY

The immortality of the soul was a central concept in Western civilization until the biblical theology movement attacked and rejected the idea. Plato was often viewed as having said something similar to what the Bible said until theologians decided that the name "Plato" was a swear word, an obscenity. Like most biblical scholars, I would rather be accused of being an ax murderer than of being a follower of Plato. In 1713 Joseph Addison wrote:

> Plato, thou reasonest well!
> Else whence this pleasing hope, this fond desire,
> This longing after immortality?
> Or whence this secret dread, and inward horror,
> Of falling into naught? Why shrinks the soul
> Back on herself, and startles at destruction?[1]

After the publication of Oscar Cullmann's 1958 essay, every theologian who was well trained was expected to condemn Platonic immortality as being the opposite of the Bible.[2] For example, Werner Jaeger, writing in the *Harvard Theological Review* in 1959, proposed that the immortal soul was a bizarre idea invented by Plato and not found anywhere in the Bible. It was allegedly imported into Christianity by the church fathers.[3] That theory of the soul became the dominant theory among theologians until twentieth-century scholars like Jaeger rescued us from that alleged error.

Theologians need not be reminded of the history of the twentieth century, which we know so well—a history in which the word "soul" was rejected by most of the top church leaders because it was thought to be a misleading word that suggested a soul-body dualism allegedly absent from the Bible. Allegedly the Hebrew concept of the whole, unified, and indivisible human was found throughout both testaments.[4] For this reason the term "soul" was often omitted from twentieth-century translations of the Bible.

No doubt there were good reasons for the crusade against the soul. Apparently there were a lot of Christian Platonists back in the old days, just as there were giant ground sloths wandering around South America until ten thousand years ago, as big as elephants and as ferocious as saber-toothed tigers. But I doubt that it is any more rational to continue a crusade against the

Platonists than against the giant ground sloths, because both are extinct today.

Where are we today? There are two groups. One group consists of Bible experts and theologians, who generally say that soul-body dualism is not found anywhere in the Bible, and that the immortality of the soul is an idea best left in the trash can, where Oscar Cullmann deposited it. Lay people and the general public, on the other hand, are quite interested in the soul, and have never heard the official party line about how dualism is unbiblical. Thomas Moore's books on the soul have been on the *New York Times* best-seller list an unbelievable number of years, which, in the eyes of many top theologians, proves that the lay public is as misguided as ever.[5]

As I have said, the notion of human wholeness, with its implication of total extinction when the body dies, is popular among most secular mental health professionals, many physicians, and most secular humanists. It does not lend itself easily to humor, nor does it lead to levity, frivolity, or hilarity. Our ancestors would have considered us to be absurd, asserting as we do that there is no soul-body dualism in the Bible, and simultaneously asserting that humans do not perish with the body. Why is this absurd? Because it is a total contradiction to which we are somehow blind. Our ancestors could see easily that which we are unable to see—namely, that if humans are so constructed as to come apart at death, with only the physical part disintegrating, then soul-body dualism in the Bible is implied.

Even if we go from a mortal body to an immortal one at the instant of death, soul-body dualism is still implied, because we do not perish when the mortal body dies. If the terminus of human life is something other than being planted six feet under, then there is dualism in the Bible, because even a child can count to two, using one finger to count the part planted six feet under and the second finger to count what is not planted six feet under. Two fingers makes dualism.

Dualism has gotten a bad name because theologians unfairly equate it with Platonism. Platonism is a bad example of dualism. All that dualism means is that there are two parts, a dichotomy. There is no inherent implication that one part is superior and the other despised (skeptics should look up "dualism" in an ordinary dictionary). The only implication is that a human life does not terminate six feet below the ground in a coffin. Platonism is like a bad marriage. The Bible presents a good marriage of body and soul, but it is still a marriage of two parts and thus implies dualism. The nonphysical part could be called "soul" or "spirit."

MINIMUM REQUIREMENTS FOR LEVITY

What is a minimum requirement for levity? Humor withers in the face of injustice, because injustice stirs up feelings of anger that are incompatible with anything other than sarcasm, which is not particularly funny.

The survival of the human spirit is not simply an expendable part of Christianity or of Judaism. This is not an optional doctrine that we can shrug off with "Maybe yes, maybe no." Without the concept of the soul there is an insoluble problem of theodicy. Omit from your religion the survival and ultimate just reward of the human spirit, and you end up with a humorless religion in which God is not very nice. I heard of a man who did not believe in the afterlife. He said that there was bad news and good news. The bad news was that God was a sadist. The good news was that God had no power.

The fourth book of Maccabees is an uplifting and inspiring book because the apparent theodicy is reversed. King Antiochus IV tortures and kills seven brothers. Evil appears to win over good. This sounds like a gruesome picture, a picture as horrifying as what I see every day in the hospital treating patients disintegrating from AIDS, diabetes, and cancer. Yet 4 Maccabees is an uplifting book. It produces a sense of euphoria, not a feeling that "life is hard and then you die." Why? The reason is that the immortal soul immediately obtains a reward in heaven. Thus the apparent theodicy is reversed. God makes King Antiochus IV into a laughing stock. He who laughs last, laughs best.

The same theme is found in the four Gospels. Jesus, the son of God, is killed despite his innocence, in what the Gospel writers regarded as the greatest miscarriage of justice in history. Not very funny. I have never been able to understand why Good Friday is called "Good." Every Good Friday I get depressed. But the tables are turned by Sunday, when God makes laughing stocks out of all those who laughed at Jesus. Even death itself dies, which, to tell you the truth, is pretty funny.

I am saying that the only solutions to theodicy are fairness and justice, and that fairness and justice usually are possible only if we endorse the afterlife. Theodicy happens and is unexplainable at the time. Having had my share of unexplained horror in my life, I don't mean to minimize the idea that bad things happen to good people like Job, without explanation at the time. However, what is the ultimate outcome? My personal experience is that in the long run I have been able to see that God is trustworthy, faithful, true, just, and fair to me and to those I love. This is not evident at the time when the horrors occur, but it becomes evident in the long run. And the Bible supports this idea, that if we endure apparent theodicy during this life, eventually—perhaps at the Day of Judgment, perhaps in heaven—we will discover that God is always as the Bible says: trustworthy, merciful, and just. Wait patiently for God's justice, the Good Book says. God's justice is one of the central themes of the Bible, and were we to say that we experience our lives as ultimately unjust and unfair, we would be rejecting the Bible.

Physicians face theodicy daily, and can do so only by means of an unconscious self-deception in regard to immortality. Immortality is apparently a lie in at least three different ways. First, it is a lie that doctors are immortal in the sense that they are immune from the diseases they treat. Second, the biblical theology movement decided that it is a lie that the immortal soul is found in the Bible. And third, the death of the idea of immortality is a lie, because the idea persists everywhere around us, and we need only listen to lay people to find that it is a biblical idea. Moreover, there is the paradoxical juxtaposition of the suffering of this life and the comfort and reward available to the faithful in the next. Chronically ill and deteriorating patients speak often of the immortal soul and of the future hope that is the anchor of their dignity in the face of the unspeakable indignities of disease (Heb. 6:19; see also Rev. 22:2–3). The theodicy of disease is balanced by the fairness that lies ahead.

CASE HISTORIES

Humor creates a sense of transcendence. If reality is ultimately paradoxical, and if what appears to be real is in some ways absurd, the stage is set for frivolity. An appreciation of the soul brings mirth, because even in one's self-concept one is partly sheltered from the sadness and tragedy of life.

For example, Frank Fabiano, a forty-five-year-old man who works as a unit clerk at my hospital, is cheerful despite four recent massive heart attacks, bypass surgery, nineteen years of back pain, and five back surgeries. Despite the fact that he is a relatively young man, Frank's days are numbered. The key to his good humor is that he says he accepts whatever is given by God. If he dies, he figures, he will go to a better place. Frank brings sunshine to an otherwise dreary hospital floor.

Within medicine in our society the dominant view of human nature is psychological—i.e., secular. That perspective offers no vision of transcendence of this life. Humor is viewed as a "defense" against reality rather than a clearer portrayal of reality. By contrast, the Christian concept of the soul brings an awareness of life after death. We are made of stuff that cannot be destroyed: God's breath and image. There are hilarious paradoxes. For example, powerful doctors are weak, whereas frail souls such as Frank display God's strength. Nearing death, Frank remains buoyant and witty.

Humor comes in two varieties. There is light humor that flits across the scene like Jerry Seinfeld in a zippy sports car, or there is industrial-strength humor that is able to move boulders. The doctrine of the soul is industrial strength.

Allow me to illustrate. My second child and first son was born in 1977 after what had appeared to be a normal pregnancy. The baby, named Justin, was born with devastating birth defects. He had no usable legs, and no bony structures below the rib cage. He even had ambiguous genitals so that the doctors needed to do six hours of genetic analysis before they could tell us whether the baby was male or female. It was clear from the first time I met Justin that he would never be able to crawl, walk, or even sit up, because he lacked the necessary bones. Furthermore, it was clear that Justin would never be toilet trained because of nerve damage to the lower spinal cord. It was unlikely that Justin would ever be welcome at any school.

This raised the question addressed in the book of Job: Who had sinned? Was it me, my wife, or God? A great deal of anger was generated by theodicy. When children are deformed, are seriously ill, or die, it is the most unacceptable horror. Upon the birth of my son Justin, the stage was not set for humor. Yet humor and levity were eventually restored.

As it happened, Justin had other birth defects, such as the absence of an aortic arch. The aorta is the big artery coming off the heart. His was missing. Justin's prognosis was death at an early age because of congestive heart failure. Indeed, at age three weeks, Justin died.

So far this does not seem to be an incident that fits easily into a chapter on levity. It is a heavy subject, a massive boulder, as anyone who has lost a child knows. How could this sad episode be used to demonstrate that the concept of the soul allows our religion to move boulders by sheer force of levity?

My wife and I were relieved, in truth, to hear that Justin was going to die. We loved the child, and would never have done anything to harm him. It was evident, however, that we were not equipped to care for so severely crippled a child, and that God could take better care of Justin—and even heal his deformities.

A few days before Justin's death, we held a baptismal service at the hospital, led by our pastor. As part of that service we sang an old slave song, "I got shoes, you got shoes, all God's children got shoes; when I get to heaven I'm gonna put on my shoes and walk all over God's heaven." No doubt this song was written by slaves with no shoes, to celebrate the paradox that a different kind of day was coming. In the case of Justin, it was a totally paradoxical song, because it captured the contradiction that he had no legs and no feet, yet we were singing about him walking all over God's heaven. We cried buckets of tears while we sang.

Is this a life of tragedy, chronic illness, and birth defects? Earlier I mentioned a dream I had in which Justin assured me that I didn't have to worry about him. In that dream, Justin was walking. Apparently, if my dream can be accepted as an imaginative interpretation of "reality," Justin has shoes, feet, and legs, and has been healed. Against all odds, and contrary to anything I learned in medical school, it is reasonable to sing: "Justin got shoes, you got shoes, all God's children got shoes; when we get to heaven we're gonna put on our shoes and walk all over God's heaven." Obviously, a dream does not carry the force of reality. But such is Christian hope.

Recently I was talking with a woman who spoke of how unacceptable she had found the death of her only son, who had died many years before, at age twenty-one. I was overwhelmed by the tragedy of her loss, and I could think of nothing helpful to say. Eventually I mustered the courage to ask her whether she believed in heaven. She replied that she did, and that she knew her son had survived death, because she could sense his presence in the room every day urging her to take courage and fight the good fight. She is a highly anxious woman who has a tendency to give up on life, except that her imaginative interactions with her son's spirit give her the buoyancy she needs to carry on, day after day. He also appears to her in dreams. I cannot tell you, nor can you tell me, whether these experiences are "real" or "imaginary." The point is that they are buoyant and allow her to be lifted out of the anxious depression she tends to sink into daily, so that she can continue her pilgrimage of faith.

Had I not been interested in the soul, I might not have asked her about her belief in heaven and thus might not have discovered that this is one of the most important features of her life. I would have been left with the impression that she had suffered an unspeakable tragedy.

The Bottom Line

So what is the bottom line? The bottom line is that the old slave spiritual has a force of reality that cannot be denied. Those without shoes will be joined by those without legs, walking all over God's heaven. It has within it the power to convert theodicy into victory, and to move boulders to mirth. The stones would cry out, Jesus told the Pharisees (Luke 19:40). I think the stones would not only cry out, but would also laugh at the paradox that frail humans, with God's help, can triumph over the horrors of disease and death.

The tragedy and unfair suffering that a physician sees daily are not all of reality, and therefore human dignity is not eroded, whittled down, nor depleted by disease, because reality is paradoxical. If one's foot dies and is amputated, if one's kidneys fail and one goes blind, if the so-called whole, unified person theologians love to talk about is whittled down so that the person is no longer whole or unified, what is left to preserve the dignity of human existence is the immortal core, because we carry inside us God's breath and image, and nothing can destroy God's breath and image. The barefoot slaves end up with shoes in heaven while their slave owner suffers the fate of the rich man roasting in the flames, begging poor Lazarus for a drop of water to cool his tongue (Luke 16:24). My innocent baby, Justin, born with no legs and no aorta, lives and walks. For all I know, he may have met Jesus face-to-face and therefore Justin may have a better father than I could ever have been to him. After more than a decade of agony, I know the answer to the question, "Why was Justin born with no legs?" The answer is not that I sinned, nor that my deceased wife sinned, nor that God sinned. The answer is given in John 9:2–3. Justin was born with no legs so that the power of God might be displayed in giving him shoes to walk all over heaven.

Horror is transformed by the alchemy of the Bible into humor. Malignancy is turned to mirth. Gravity is turned to levity. If you doubt that gravity is turned to levity, contemplate 1 Thessalonians 4:17, in which Paul says that we will be caught up together with the church triumphant in the clouds to meet God in the air. Gravity will be demoted and levity promoted.

This is not the zippy little sports car brand of humor. This is industrial-strength wit, capable of shattering the heaviest boulders that have ever crushed the human spirit into frivolous and temporary pebbles in our relationship with God. If, when Christ emerged from the tomb, death itself died, then so did theodicy. And if theodicy died, then so did humorlessness.

Conclusion

Human nature is fundamentally paradoxical. In creating us, God built a contradiction into the core, into the heart, of the beast—a contradiction that Jesus declared often:

- Those who seek their life will lose it;
- Those who lose their life for Christ will find it.

This paradox is absolutely central to human nature. The tendency in secular culture is for people to seek their lives—to seek to fulfill their potential, satisfy their needs, indulge their cravings, and optimize their lifestyles. What life is all about, many say, is being happy.

My clinical experience has shown me that the search for secular "happiness" is the road to moral poverty and disappointment. It is not the road to compassion for those who are indigent, despairing, or hopeless. When Jesus said the self-indulgent will lose their *life,* he meant it in the sense of the Greek word *psyche*, which is translated "life" but refers also to "self" or "soul." In other words, those who seek to find themselves, to find the vitality of life, will lose the very thing they seek. Put another way, those who seek self-esteem will not find it, but will taste the bitter herbs of disappointment. People don't expect a psychiatrist to say something like this.

Years ago while waiting in line to buy a cup of coffee in the cafeteria of the last hospital I worked in, I noticed the man who was then president of the hospital standing behind me. Offering polite conversation, as we dug two quarters out of our pockets, he asked how my books were selling. I asked if he would like to buy one. He laughed, smiled, and said, "No, we hospital administrators don't read books on the soul. I sold my soul to the devil years ago." I enjoyed his lighthearted humor.

Why "Soul"?

In a self-centered age, it is important to present the gospel in a self-centered format. This may sound like a contradiction, but it is not, because the "soul" is paradoxical. It is the perfect word for apologetic purposes, because it means precisely what the word "self" would mean if one were to take off the secular blinders and look at oneself with an open mind. Human nature is much richer and more colorful than secular psychotherapists acknowledge.

God's breath and image are found inside us, so there is something of infinite value in everyone. The soul is the animating energy that motivates us. According to the Bible, that energy resides in a person's breath, which comes from God: "It is the spirit in a mortal, the breath of the Almighty, that makes for understanding" (Job 32:8). The soul is richer than the secular "self" because it focuses our attention on our potential union with Christ, values such as self-denial or loving one's enemies, prayer, human depravity, rebellion against God, our survival of death, and the upcoming judgment by Christ.

In a self-absorbed age, the path of self-absorption can be exploited by evangelists talking about the soul. Is it in a person's interest to gain the whole world but lose his or her soul? Is it wise to plan for the future but fail to recognize the judgment that future contains? Can those who seek self-fulfillment say that they are happy without God?

The pollster George Gallup has prophesied that the church of the future will belong to the laity much more than the church

TABLE 3 LOSS OF MEMBERSHIP IN
MAINSTREAM DENOMINATIONS
(IN MILLIONS AND PERCENT OF U.S. POPULATION)

	1960	1990
UCC	2.2 (1.25%)	1.6 (0.64%)
Episcopal	3.3 (1.82%)	2.4 (0.98%)
Presbyterian	4.2 (2.32%)	2.8 (1.14%)
Methodist	10.6 (5.93%)	8.9 (3.58%)
Lutheran	5.3 (2.95%)	5.2 (2.11%)

of today.[1] Those leaders who listen to lay people with respect will prosper.[2] The power in tomorrow's church will flow from the bottom up, not from the top down, Gallup predicts. This has implications for the doctrine of the soul, because lay people are far more interested in the soul than are clergy and theologians.

Psychiatrists and religious leaders choke on the word "soul." But "soul" is an amazing word. It defines what is missing in our society. It is a word we can use only if we tear down the psychological/spiritual distinction, which is precisely why we need it.

Of course, if we were to say that secular psychotherapists treat the soul, we would capture everyone's attention. It sounds outrageous. No one would assume that secular psychotherapists are competent to treat the soul. But where does the outrage lie? Is the statement outrageous because it is wrong, or because it is accurate? I claim it is the latter.

In the United States the secular mental health movement is vast and growing, whereas mainline churches are dwindling. Between 1960 and 1990 there was a dramatic decline in membership of United Church of Christ, Episcopal, Presbyterian, and United Methodist churches, both in absolute numbers and in percentage of the U.S. population, as shown in Table 3.[3] This decline began about 1960, which is immediately after New Testament scholars finished discrediting the soul. (According to a recent study by sociologist Kirk Hadaway, however, in the early 1990s the Episcopal church has returned to growth.[4]) But, of course, there is no proof of a causal connection.[5] Psychothera-

107

pists offer treatment of the soul while theologians are in total disarray about the soul. Therapists have abundant work and long waiting lists; pews of liberal churches are half-filled. How ironic. Clergy send their parishioners off to secular humanist psychotherapists like shepherds sending their sheep to wolves.

THEOLOGY OF THE SOUL

Within the esoteric world of biblical scholarship, the soul was devalued because it was thought to be too Platonic. When we say that it is essential to embrace the soul again, and to put the word "soul" back into future translations of the Bible, we are not just talking about semantics. We are discussing the fundamental teaching of the Bible: human nature and its regeneration. It is erroneous to say that the Bible teaches the same view of humans as secular psychotherapists espouse.

On no subject is this more hotly debated than on the translation of Genesis 2:7. God creates Adam from dust, and breathes into his nostrils the breath of life. If one believes the "humans-as-whole-people" interpretation, one avoids the word "soul" in that verse, as every single twentieth-century translation has done.[6] Most hold that Adam "became a living being," thereby emphasizing the "human-as-whole-person."

What is the alternative approach? In many places the Bible emphasizes a dichotomous view of human nature. Ecclesiastes 12:7 says that at death, "the dust returns to the earth as it was, and the breath returns to God who gave it" (NRSV). The underlying idea is that humans consist of a clay body and an inner part that is subjectivity, mind, understanding, which is the Spirit that God blew into us. The ghost of the prophet Samuel comes up from Sheol to talk with King Saul after Samuel's body has died (1 Sam. 28:13–20). This duality of body and spirit lends credibility to the traditional translation of Genesis 2:7, which says that Adam "became a living soul" (KJV).

I am suggesting that the Hebrew words can be translated either way. Every translation involves interpretation. In this century, most translators have opted for a "humans-as-whole-people" interpretation. The translation of Genesis 2:7 that is most consistent with the biblical theme of a dichotomous human nature is the King James Version—Adam "became a living soul," which was how the verse was understood by Jews at the time of Jesus.

The following verses demonstrate that Jews at the time of Jesus had a dualistic understanding of Genesis 2:7:

> And gavest a body unto Adam without soul, which was the workmanship of thine hands, and didst breathe into him the breath of life, and he was made living before thee. (2 Esd. 3:5–6 KJV)
>
> Their heart is in ashes, their hope is cheaper than dirt, and their lives are of less worth than clay, because they failed to know the one who formed them and inspired them with active souls and breathed a living spirit into them. (Wisd. of Sol. 15:10–11 NRSV)

Thus, whatever Genesis 2:7 meant originally, by the time of Jesus it tended to be interpreted by Jews as implying a dichotomous human nature.

PARADIGM SHIFT

The philosopher Thomas Kuhn has written of paradigm shifts in science.[7] I propose a paradigm shift with respect to our understanding of human nature. The old scientific paradigm rejects the soul because it is "unscientific." We need a new paradigm that endorses the soul as the cornerstone of our anthropology. The whole Bible could be understood as being focused on the soul, because the Bible is the story of how humans (i.e., souls) responded to God.

According to the scientific paradigm for understanding human experience, God's existence cannot be proved. Therefore the soul is also vulnerable to being discredited. Furthermore, as William Barrett has shown in his book *Death of the Soul*, without the soul humans are viewed as if they were mere computers, lacking all those characteristics that are uniquely human, such as creative reasoning, ethical decision making, and judgments based on values, goals, meaning, and purpose.

A recent cover of *Time* trumpeted the following headline: "In Search of the Mind: Scientists Peer into the Brain Looking for That Evanescent Thing Called Consciousness." According to this report, "a memory is nothing more than a few thousand brain cells firing in a particular, established pattern. . . . Consciousness may be an evanescent illusion."[8] Will we begin to doubt our own experience of being conscious?

There is a potential domino effect: if God doesn't exist, the soul doesn't exist; if the soul doesn't exist, the human mind loses its mystery and integrity. A scientific approach that rejects the soul has little room for any subjective or inner experience such as prayer or contemplation.

In order to affirm that humans exist, we have invented pseudosciences such as psychotherapy. These disciplines claim to be part of the scientific tradition, but most physicists and other hard scientists scoff at the idea of psychotherapy being a science. A majority of biological psychiatrists say that there is not the slightest hint of science in Freud's teachings.[9] "Science" has become a bandwagon many scholars want to jump onto—especially biblical scholars and theologians. In the process, the inner experience of human life has been devalued. For example, dreams and visions are central to the Bible, being one of the primary channels through which God spoke to God's people, especially to the prophets. Yet dreams and visions are almost never mentioned in theology today, because they don't fit the paradigm of "science." This lack of emphasis on inner life has had an impact on how we study the Bible.

Traditionally, Scripture was read in a manner different from what is accepted in many academic seminaries today. It was said that only with inspiration by the Holy Spirit could one read and comprehend Scripture. Thus the Bible was read prayerfully. People meditated upon and contemplated the biblical metaphors, seeking in the Spirit to understand inner or deeper meanings of the biblical images. They understood Scripture the way one makes tea: by putting a biblical passage into the water of one's inner life and letting it steep, so that one's soul infuses the Scripture, and the Scripture diffuses through one's soul. Even in the Bible, when New Testament writers read the Old Testament, they read Scripture in this time-honored method. Such an approach would never be accepted in a theological research journal today—again, because it is not "scientific."

The allegedly "scientific" direction of biblical scholarship is related also to the lack of psychological insight into the Bible. James Barr once said something to me that I've never forgotten: "In general, biblical scholars have not gone in a psychological direction in their scholarship. And someday there is going to be a terrible price that will have to be paid for that failure."[10]

But I am convinced that we are in the midst of a paradigm shift. The age of science—one that ignores religious sensibilities—is drawing to a close. The age of the Spirit is dawning. Within the age of the Spirit it will be essential to emphasize the soul, to understand the Bible as the greatest psychiatry textbook ever written.[11]

One of the great mathematicians in the world today, Benoit Mandelbrot of Yale University and IBM, once told me: "Things are predictable in theory, but in fact we find that they are not predictable. There is this element of randomness that comes in when you deal with the real world." Mandelbrot added that in the old days, science had determinism with a certain amount of static around the edges, a certain amount of fuzziness that the determinism couldn't explain. Now, he claims, "we have a second stage of science, the stage of indeterminism."[12]

This reflects the paradigm shift I am addressing. No absolutes. Confusion. MTV. The popularity of chaos theory is a prime example. Chaos Theory undermines the fundamental assumption of the public's trust in science—namely, that we live in a world in which science can make reliable prophecies.[13] Thus from the viewpoint of science, the physical world is predictable only half the time—and that leaves a lot of room for miracles.

Christians should strike while the iron is hot. Scientific determinism can no longer be trusted—but the Bible can. This is why churches that emphasize the Bible, such as evangelical churches, are growing.[14] Churches deemphasizing the Bible are shrinking fast. As a whole, mainline Protestant churches have nowhere near the membership that they had a few decades ago.

If one accepts this view of a paradigm shift, many new possibilities come into view. Today the soul is the most urgently needed idea in America. Only if God exists is there a basis for talking about the soul. But the incredible transformation in our thinking does not stop there. It has the potential to illuminate even our biological research. This is evident in our understanding of DNA. Even DNA has both a soul (meaning, purpose) and a body (physical structure), as discussed in chapter 1.

All biologists recognize the need to use language that implies purpose when describing biological systems, even mindless systems. They might remark, "The goals of this nest-building behavior of sparrows are escape from predators and warmth for the winter." Yet whose ultimate purposes are they describing? To explore this question would be considered unscientific. The limits of science, unfortunately, are narrow.

To discuss the soul adequately, we need to adopt a humble attitude. We will never understand all of what it means to be human. Further, it is a monumental undertaking to try to gather information about the soul that is available from modern medicine, the Bible, and all of history. This book has been only a preliminary sketch of some of what could be said about the soul.

Fundamentally, we do not need to understand everything about the soul. We need only to understand the orientation of the soul. Everything else is extraneous claptrap, bells and whistles that add nothing.

The soul can be oriented in only two ways: toward self-fulfillment or toward God. American culture and the secular mental health movement teach self-fulfillment—the "gospel of self-esteem," as if the soul could puff itself up like a self-inflating balloon. American culture teaches that self-flattery can produce miracles.

The other orientation, toward God, is not possible unless the soul is reborn. What this means is that God's spirit comes in and merges with the soul, and slowly transforms it and makes it a new creation (Col. 3:9–10; Rom. 8:5–16).

The soul is not an end in itself. When someone asks me, "How do I find my soul?" I reply, "Don't look for it. Your soul will be discovered indirectly if you follow these two goals:

1. Love God with all your heart, and with all your soul, and with all your mind;

2. Love your neighbor as yourself." *(Matt. 22:37–39, Mark 12:30–31, Luke 10:27)*

My fundamental teaching is not about locating the soul, but about the orientation of the soul. We should be less interested in human nature than in human purpose—the goal (*telos*) toward which our lives are directed. The purpose of life consists of these two goals, which are not taught by secular psychotherapists. And that is the full extent of my complaint against the mental health movement.

RECOVERY—AND CHRISTIAN HOPE

Let me conclude with a case history.[15] Leslie Dickerson had a devastating childhood. She felt unloved and unlovable as far back as she could remember. Emptiness, inner deadness, lack of self-worth, and painful rejection—these were the feelings she experienced in her soul, at the deepest level. She suffered rejection by her parents as well, and their rejection was the picture of them that she carried within her soul. As she grew up, she began to attempt suicide and to abuse alcohol and drugs. She was torn by rage, depression, and anxiety.

Eventually Leslie fell into the mental health treatment system, and she failed to improve with every known treatment: long-term intensive psychotherapy, family therapy, every known medication, and electric shock treatment. She suffered from the most untreatable of psychiatric conditions, borderline personality disorder. For a decade she was in and out of psychiatric hospitals. One time she spent three years continuously in a state mental hospital, misdiagnosed as schizophrenic. Her therapists all gave up on her as untreatable.

One day she gave birth to a daughter, and suddenly knew that she had a choice of either changing her life or losing the baby—if she didn't reorder her life, the state social workers would intervene. The dilemma motivated her to search more desperately than ever for a solution to her problems. Finally, she turned to Jesus Christ for the first time in her life, and prayed for forgiveness. For the first time ever, she felt accepted, she felt lovable, and peace such as she had never before experienced flooded her heart.

From that day forward, Leslie never again attempted suicide. As she took root in this new soil, a profound psychological reorganization occurred. It was based on the experience of feeling forgiven and accepted at her core. As bad as she thought she was, it had all been overcome at Calvary. Her badness, she said, had been washed away by the Blood of the Lamb.

Leslie has now been happy and free of psychiatrists for ten years. She works as an administrative assistant at a large doctors' office, and is devoted to her two children and to her church. Her favorite name for God is "The Great Psychiatrist." She has positive memories of the psychiatrists that used to try to help her, but she claims they did not have the medicine she needed. Before her conversion she had been haunted by an occasional auditory hallucination, and a paranoid dread of closed doors. Since her conversion she has been free of these psychotic symptoms, without any medication.

Leslie speaks of inviting Jesus into her heart. For more than an hour every morning, before her children wake up, she sits alone in a room and talks with Jesus, whom she calls her best friend. The conversation, she says, goes both ways. She prays about something, and a specific Bible verse then occurs to her. Reading this verse, she interprets it to be Jesus' reply to her prayer.

I asked Leslie how she can tell that a certain idea is what Jesus wants her to do, rather than her own thought. She said there are three criteria:

1. The idea is consistent with what the Bible says.

2. The idea fits her life circumstances.

3. Peace and tranquillity come into her life after the decision is made.

After she met Jesus, she discovered that her parents were quite different than she had thought they were. She now sees that they were the best parents they were capable of being. She has reestablished a loving relationship with both of them. In retrospect, she has discovered that her misperception of her mother as a malignant person was based on the experience of being sickly as an infant, so that the infant-mother relationship had gotten off on the wrong track. Although for many years she experienced her mother as "a bad mother," the fact is that she had a decent mother who tried the best she could to care for an infant that could not be comforted.

Leslie speaks of taking Jesus into her heart, so that he dwells inside her. Jesus brought Leslie such a feeling of being accepted that she finally relaxed. Seeking a new relationship with her mother, she discovered that her mother had more to offer than she had ever imagined, and this led to a healing of their relationship. Jesus, she claims, also healed her self-esteem. "I used to be a mouse," she says. "Now I roar like a lion."

In all my years as a psychiatrist, I have met only one person who ever truly recovered from borderline personality disorder. Her name is Leslie Dickerson.

NOTES

INTRODUCTION

1. Krister Stendahl, "Immortality Is Too Much and Too Little," in *Meanings: The Bible as Document and Guide* (Minneapolis: Augsburg Fortress Press, 1984), 193–202. Stendahl subsequently changed his view when I asked him to write a book with me endorsing the soul. See Preface and Comments chapters of Jeffrey H. Boyd, *Affirming the Soul: Remarkable Conversations between Mental Health Professionals and an Ordained Minister* (Cheshire, Conn.: Soul Research Institute, 1994).

2. Jeffrey H. Boyd, "Losing Soul: How and Why Theologians Created the Mental Health Movement," *Calvin Theological Journal* 30 (November 1995): 472–92; Boyd, "Mental Health Professionals and the Soul," *Journal of Psychology and Theology* 23 (fall 1995): 151–60; Boyd, "On Use of the Term Soul," *Journal of Psychology and Theology* 23 (fall 1995): 161–70; Boyd, "One's Self-Concept and Biblical Theology," *Journal of the Evangelical Theological Society*, in press; Boyd, "Apocalypse from Nuclear War Compared with the Expected Apocalypse of October 22, 1844," *Henceforth* (in press); and Boyd, "Where Is the Soul in the Midst of All This Medical Technology?", presented at the Yale Program for the Humanities in Medicine, Yale Medical School, New Haven, Conn., 13 April 1995.

3. Susan Pearsall, "The Rev. Dr. Jeffrey H. Boyd: Psychiatrist and Explorer of the Soul," *New York Times*, Connecticut section, 12 March 1995, CN 3.

4. The Greek word ψυχή can be transliterated *psyche* or *psuche*.

5. Jeffrey H. Boyd, *Soul Psychology: How to Understand Your Soul in Light of the Mental Health Movement* (Cheshire, Conn.: Soul Research Institute, 1994), 336–37, n. 77; Bruno Bettelheim, *Freud*

and Man's Soul (New York: Random House, 1984); and Bettelheim, "Reflections: Freud and the Soul," *New Yorker,* 1 March 1982, 52–93. Freud said of the German word *Seele*:

> *Psyche* is a Greek word and translates into German as soul (German: *Seele*). Treatment of the psyche means therefore treatment of the soul (*Seelenbehandlung*). One could also understand it to mean treatment of sickness when it occurs in the life of the soul (*Seelenlebens*). (Translation by the author.)

Sigmund Freud, "Psychische Behandlung (Seelenbehandlung)," ["Treatment of the Psyche (Treatment of the Soul)"], in *Die Gesundheit,* ed. R. Kossmann and J. Weiss (Stuttgart, Berlin, and Leipzig: Union Deutsche Verlagsgesellschaft, 1905), vol. 1, 368–84.

6. Boyd, "Losing Soul"; Boyd, "On Use of the Term 'Soul,'" *Journal of Psychology and Theology* 23 (fall 1995): 151–60; Boyd, "Mental Health Professionals and 'the Soul,'" *Journal of Psychology and Theology* 23 (fall 1995): 161–70; and Boyd, *Affirming the Soul.*

7. *American Psychiatric Association Task Force Report 10: Psychiatrists' Viewpoints on Religion and Their Services to Religious Institutions and the Ministry* (Washington, D.C.: American Psychiatric Association, 1975); Claude Ragan, H. Newton Malony, and Benjamin Bert-Hallahmi, "Psychologists and Religion: Professional Factors and Personal Belief," *Review of Religious Research* 21 (spring 1980): 208–17. In Ragan et al., Table 2 on p. 212 shows that 17 percent of psychologists were "orthodox" in ideology and another 26 percent were somewhat orthodox. At the bottom of the page, the text adds together these two percentages, and arrives at 43 percent believing in God. The article shows that psychologists are much less religious than academics in general, and than the American public. [David B. Larson, E. Mansell Pattison, Dan G. Blazer, et al., "Systematic Analysis of Research on Religious Variables in Four Major Psychiatric Journals 1978–1982," *American Journal of Psychiatry* 143 (1986): 329–34. On p. 329 they incorrectly quote an unpublished study of Ragan et al. in 1976 that found that 5 percent of the psychologists in the APA believe in God.]

8. Gallup Poll, *Religion in America: The Gallup Report #259* (April 1987). Whereas 87 percent of Americans are certain that Jesus literally rose from the dead, only 30 percent of mental health experts believe so. See W. E. Henry, J. H. Sims, and S. L. Spray, *The Fifth Profession* (San Francisco: Jossey-Bass, 1971), 45–71.

9. Albert Ellis, "Psychotherapy and Atheistic Values: A Re-

sponse to A. Bergin's 'Psychotherapy and Religious Values,'" *Journal of Consulting and Clinical Psychology* 48 (1980): 635–39.

10. L. Rebecca Propst, Richard Ostrom, Philip Watkins, Terri Dean, and David Mashburn, "Comparative Efficacy of Religious and Nonreligious Cognitive-Behavioral Therapy for the Treatment of Clinical Depression in Religious Individuals," *Journal of Consulting and Clinical Psychology* 60 (1992): 94–103.

11. The three paragraphs preceding this note come from ideas expressed in Gordon R. Lewis's letter of September 30, 1995, and also found in his book *Integrative Theology*.

12. In the city of New Haven, Connecticut, the *Yellow Pages* of 1994–95 show that there are 60 percent more listings for psychotherapists than for churches and synagogues. In other words, if you add together all the Protestant, Catholic, and Jewish denominations, there are 340 churches and synagogues listed. There are 555 listings for mental health experts offering psychotherapy: 192 for marriage and family therapists, 48 for social workers, 132 for psychologists, 69 for psychotherapists, and 114 for psychiatrists. These figures do not include an additional 7 listings under the heading of Child Guidance, 30 under Drug Abuse and Addiction, and 41 under Alcoholism.

In every city the author has studied, the *Yellow Pages* indicate that psychotherapists outnumber churches and synagogues. For example, in the city of Syracuse, New York, there are 433 listings for churches and synagogues, but 448 listings for mental health professionals offering psychotherapy. (*NYNEX Yellow Pages*, Syracuse Metropolitan Area, May 1994–April 1995).

13. Mental health and chemical dependency treatment represents about 15 percent of the health care dollar (about 8 or 9 percent for mental health, and the other 6 or 7 percent for chemical dependency). About 14 percent of the American gross domestic product goes toward health care—i.e., about $526 billion in annual health care costs as of the mid-1990s. Multiply the two numbers (15 percent times 14 percent) and you get 2.1 percent. The percentage of the gross domestic product devoted to health care has been rising rapidly: until the last year or two it was rising at 1 percent per year! [Bentson H. McFarland, "Cost-Effectiveness Considerations for Managed Care Systems: Treating Depression in Primary Care," *American Journal of Medicine* 97 (suppl. 6A) (December 19, 1994): 6A–48S; see also Kenneth L. Minaker, "The Changing Face of Health Care for the Elderly," paper presented at the Con-

ference on Geriatric Psychiatry, Harvard Medical School, Boston, Mass., September 29, 1995.]

14. The American gross domestic product in 1993 was $6,343.8 billion, according to the U.S. Census Bureau. The health care industry consumes 14 percent of that, and mental health and substance abuse 15 percent of that. Multiplying those three numbers, the result is $133.2. This has risen from an estimated $129 billion in 1988. [See D. A. Wasylenki, "The Cost of Schizophrenia," *Canadian Journal of Psychiatry* 39 (9 Suppl. 2) (November 1994): S65–69.] These numbers, however, are notoriously variable, depending on which numbers you use for which purpose. For example, if one counts only mental health and not chemical dependency, the percentage of the health care dollar drops to 8 or 9 percent, and if the health care budget is taken to be $526 billion per year, the resulting cost of mental health care would be $47 billion per year (see Minaker, "The Changing Face of Health Care for the Elderly"). Since economists usually include substance abuse (i.e., chemical dependency) treatment with mental health, it would seem safe to estimate that the costs are approximately twice $47 billion. Thus $100 billion per year is as safe a number as one will find, recognizing that any number has a large variance.

Capitation is rapidly taking over the American medical system, and this may reduce the amount of money spent on mental health services in the future. ("Capitation" means that insurance companies would pay a doctors group a fixed amount of money per thousand patients, and let the doctors assume the risk of cost overruns.)

The unbelievable expansion of the secular mental health movement over the last five decades may be slowed or even reversed by managed care. The changes in health care financing start in California and move eastward. From California we learn that capitation is the preferred approach to holding down costs. As capitation sweeps through the medical system, there is projected to be a vast reduction in the need for psychiatric and psychological services. Based on the assumption of capitation, there is a 74 percent oversupply of mental health professionals as of 1995. From the viewpoint of this book, that is good news, for if the American soul is no longer being cared for in the mental health system, Americans may turn to God for care of their soul. [See M. S. Jellinek and B. Nurcombe, "Two Wrongs Don't Make a Right: Managed Care, Mental Health, and the Marketplace," *Journal of the American Medical Association* 270 (1993): 1737–39; A. Lazarus, "Ten Reasons Why

Psychiatrists May Dislike Managed Competition," *Hospital and Community Psychiatry* 45 (1994): 496–98; P. J. Fink, "Psychiatrists' Role in Managed Care Programs," *Hospital and Community Psychiatry* 44 (1993): 723–24.]

15. See William J. Bennett, "Getting Used to Decadence: The Spirit of Democracy in Modern America," *Heritage Lectures* #477, December 1993.

16. The apostle Paul spoke about those who thought they could justify their life based on the resources inside themselves. He said they were trapped in a dead-end lifestyle that he called "sin" or the "old Adam." Here is how two leading Pauline scholars interpret what Paul meant by "sin":

> The ultimate sin reveals itself to be the false assumption of receiving life not as a gift of the Creator but procuring it by one's own power, of living from one's self rather than from God. [Rudolf Bultmann, "The Theology of Paul," in *Theology of the New Testament*, trans. Kendrick Grobel (London: SCM Press, 1965), vol. 1, 232.]
>
> Sin is . . . man's isolation from, his independence of, God, and his pride in his own ability to deal with life on the level of his own wisdom. . . . [the] chief disaster is that men are caught in the toils of their own little selfhood. [Alexander C. Purdy, "Paul the Apostle," in *Interpreter's Dictionary of the Bible: An Illustrated Encyclopedia*, 4 vols. plus supplement, ed. Charles A. Buttrick et al. (Nashville: Abingdon, 1981), vol. 3, 692.]

This Pauline viewpoint contradicts one of the main tendencies inside the secular mental health movement. There is a powerful trend for psychotherapists to teach that the ultimate goal of life is restoration of self-esteem, autonomy, self-fulfillment, reaching your potential, individuation, and self-reliance.

17. David F. Wells, *No Place for Truth: Or Whatever Happened to Evangelical Theology?* (Grand Rapids, Mich.: Eerdmans, 1993).

18. My view tends to disagree with theologians such as Robert Schuller, who promote self-esteem as something we need as central to the Christian religion. My own view is that our devotion to God is central, and such devotion sometimes leads to us feeling abysmal, other times to self-esteem, for our identity is that of sinners forgiven by God. [See Robert H. Schuller, *Self-Esteem: The New Reformation* (Waco, Tex.: Word Books, 1982).]

19. To avoid confusion, we need to recognize that among Jungians there is a different meaning of the word "self." They use the word as a technical name for God. The author is not a Jungian. In

this book the name "God" is used for God, and "self" takes on its common, dictionary meaning, a synonym of "myself" or "yourself." The "self" could be defined as "who I am."

20. Augustine, *Confessions,* trans. R. S. Pine-Coffin (New York: Penguin Books, 1987), 21.

21. Sigmund Freud, "Civilization and Its Discontents," in *The Standard Edition of the Complete Psychological Works of Sigmund Freud,* vol. 21, trans. James Strachey (London: Hogarth Press, 1986), 76.

22. Thomas Moore, *Care of the Soul: A Guide for Cultivating Depth and Sacredness in Everyday Life* (New York: HarperCollins, 1992); Moore, *Soul Mates: Honoring the Mysteries of Love and Relationship* (New York: HarperCollins, 1994).

23. Moore, *Care of the Soul,* xi. Moore's eloquence becomes more obvious when we compare this statement to the opening statement of Sproul's book on the soul, which reads: "Something is missing. It is missing from the life of the church." [See R. C. Sproul, *Soul's Quest for God* (Wheaton, Ill.: Tyndale, 1993), ix.]

24. Emily Yoffe, "How the Soul Is Sold: James Hillman Developed a Psychoanalytic Theory Few Could Understand, Until His Protégé Thomas Moore Translated It for the Masses," *New York Times Magazine,* 23 April 1995, 44–49; James Hillman and Michael Ventura, *We've Had a Hundred Years of Psychotherapy—and the World's Getting Worse* (San Francisco: HarperSanFrancisco, 1992); Hillman, *Kinds of Power: An Intelligent Guide to Its Uses* (New York: Doubleday, 1995); Hillman, *Anima: An Anatomy of a Personified Notion* (Dallas: Spring Publications, 1985); Hillman, *Archetypal Psychology: A Brief Account* (Dallas: Spring Publications, 1983); Hillman, *The Dream and the Underworld* (New York: HarperCollins, 1979); Hillman, *Emotion: A Comprehensive Phenomenology of Theories and Their Meanings for Therapies* (Evanston, Ill.: Northwestern University Press, 1992); Hillman, *The Myth of Analysis* (New York: HarperCollins, 1992); Hillman, *Revisioning Psychology* (New York: HarperCollins, 1992); Hillman, *Suicide and the Soul* (Dallas: Spring Publications, 1964); Hillman, *The Thought of the Heart and the Soul of the World* (Dallas: Spring Publications, 1992); Hillman, *Healing Fiction* (Barrytown, N.Y.: Station Hill Press, 1983); Hillman, *Insearch: Psychology and Religion* (Dallas: Spring Publications, 1967); Carl G. Jung, *Modern Man in Search of a Soul,* trans. W. S. Bell and Cary F. Baynes (New York: Harcourt Brace Jovanovich, 1933); and Jung, *On the Nature of the Psyche,* trans. R. F. C. Hull (Princeton, N.J.: Princeton University Press, 1960).

25. Jungian experts in theology claim that Carl Jung and the Jungian tradition are fundamentally Gnostic. See R. A. Segal, ed., *Jung: Gnostic* (Princeton, N.J.: Princeton University Press, 1992); Murray Stein, "The Gnostic Critique, Past and Present," in *The Allure of Gnosticism,* ed. R. A. Segal, J. Singer, and Murray Stein (Chicago: Open Court, 1995); David Miller, ed., *Jung and the Interpretation of the Bible* (New York: Continuum, 1995); Wayne G. Rollins, *Jung and the Bible* (Louisville: Westminster John Knox, 1983); Stein, *Jung's Treatment of Christianity: The Psychotherapy of a Religious Tradition* (Wilmette, Ill.: Chiron, 1985). At the November 1994 annual meeting of the Society of Biblical Literature in Chicago, there was an entire symposium on Jung as a Gnostic, presented by the Psychology and the Bible Group.

26. There has been a flood of new books on the soul since 1990, most of which, unfortunately, lack theological sophistication, and many of which do not come out of a Judeo-Christian tradition: Kenneth J. Collins, *Soul Care: Deliverance and Renewal through the Christian Life* (Wheaton, Ill.: Victor Books, 1995); Walter Dorherty, *Soul Searching: Why Psychotherapy Must Promote Moral Responsibility* (New York: Basic Books, 1995); David Schiedermayer, *Putting the Soul Back in Medicine: Reflections on Compassion and Ethics* (Grand Rapids, Mich.: Baker Books, 1994); Kathy Oddenino, *A Soul Approach to Depression: Our Normal Transitional Emotions* (Annapolis, Md.: Joy Publications, 1995); Elie Wiesel, *Souls on Fire: Portraits and Legends of Hasidic Masters* (Northvale, N.J.: Aronson, 1993); R. C. Sproul, *Soul's Quest for God;* Thomas Day, *Where Have You Gone, Michelangelo? The Loss of Soul in Catholic Culture* (New York: Crossroad, 1993); Jessie Penn-Lewis, *Soul and Spirit* (Fort Washington, Pa.: Christian Literature Crusade, 1993); Angela Tilby, *Soul: God, Self, and the New Cosmology* (New York: Doubleday, 1993); Phil Cousineau, ed., *Soul of the World: A Modern Book of Hours* (San Francisco: HarperSanFrancisco, 1993); Gershon Winkler, *Soul of the Matter: A Jewish-Kabbalistic Perspective on the Human Soul Before, During, and After "Life"* (Brooklyn, N.Y.: Judaica Press, 1992); Kenneth Leech, *Soul Friend: An Invitation to Spiritual Direction* (San Francisco: HarperSanFrancisco, 1992); Wayne Bloomqist, ed., *Soul and Its Powers* (Wilmot, Wis.: Lotus Light, 1992); Darlene P. Hopson, *Soul Mates* (New York: Prentice Hall, 1992); Bob Lancer, *Soulmate Process* (Malibu, Calif.: Valley Sun, 1992); William G. McLoughlin, *Soul Liberty: The Baptists' Struggle in New England, 1630–1833* (Hanover, N.H.: University Press of New England, 1991); John A. Sanford, *Soul Journey: A Jungian Analyst Looks at Reincarnation*

(New York: Crossroad, 1991); Michael Grosso, *Soul Maker: Stories from the Far Side of the Psyche* (Norfolk, Va.: Hampton Roads Publishing Co., 1991); Edward Sellner, *Soul-Making: The Telling of a Spiritual Journey* (Mystic, Conn.: Twenty-Third Publishers, 1991); Leonard Shengold, *Soul Murder: Effects of Childhood Abuse and Deprivation* (New York: Fawcett, 1991); Sandra Ingerman, *Soul Retrieval: Mending the Fragmented Self through Shamanic Practice* (San Francisco: HarperSanFrancisco, 1991); Henry H. Mitchell and Nicholas C. Lewter, *Soul Theology: The Heart of American Black Culture* (Nashville: Abingdon, 1991); C. Welton Gaddy, *Soul Under Siege: Surviving Clergy Depression* (Louisville, Ky.: Westminster John Knox, 1991); Peter Lord, *Soul Care* (Grand Rapids, Mich.: Baker Books, 1990); Alan Oken, *Soul Centered Astrology* (New York: Bantam, 1990); Rosamond Smith, *Soul-Mate* (New York: NAL-Dutton, 1990); David Lodge, *Souls and Bodies* (New York: Viking Penguin, 1990). All the books in note 25 above (Gnostic Jungians) also focus on the soul.

1. THE ORIGIN OF THE SOUL

1. Caroline W. Bynum, *The Resurrection of the Body in Western Christianity, 200–1336* (New York: Columbia University Press, 1995).

2. Charlotte Johnstone, "It's Easier to Wear Fruit on Your Head Than to Feed It to a Baby," *Family Circle,* 14 March 1995, 121.

3. Tertullian, *De Anima,* ed. J. H. Waszink (Amsterdam: J. M. Meulenhoff, 1947).

4. Jacqueline S. Sachs, "Recognition Memory for Syntactic and Semantic Aspects of Connected Discourse," *Perception and Psychophysics* 2 (February 1967): 437–42; cited in Mary S. Van Leeuwen, *The Person in Psychology: A Contemporary Christian Appraisal* (Grand Rapids, Mich.: Eerdmans, 1985), 151.

5. Noam Chomsky, *Syntactic Structures* (The Hague: Mouton, 1957).

6. James Barr, *The Semantics of Biblical Language* (Philadelphia: Trinity Press International, 1961).

7. Leslie Brothers, "A Biological Perspective on Empathy," *American Journal of Psychiatry* 146 (1989): 10–19.

8. Kenneth S. Kendler, "Overview: A Current Perspective on Twin Studies of Schizophrenia," *American Journal of Psychiatry* 140 (1983): 1413–25.

9. Boyd, *Affirming the Soul,* 117–40.

10. Azariah: Song of Three Young Men 1:40–51, from the Apocrypha, KJV.

2. The Loss of the Soul

1. Krister Stendahl, "Immortality Is Too Much," 193–202.

2. C. G. Berkouwer, *Man: The Image of God* (Grand Rapids: Eerdmans, 1962), 201, 203.

3. Reinhold Niebuhr, *The Nature and Destiny of Man: A Christian Interpretation* (New York: Charles Scribner's Sons, 1949), 5–13.

4. Boyd, "Where Is the Soul?"

5. Stendahl, *The School of Saint Matthew* (Ramsey, N.J.: Sigler Press, 1991).

6. Boyd, *Affirming the Soul*. Krister Stendahl reviewed the entire manuscript, wrote the preface, and is extensively interviewed throughout the book for his ideas about the biblical soul.

7. O. W. Heick, "If a Man Die, Shall He Live Again?" *Lutheran Quarterly* 17 (1965): 99–110; P. G. Lindhardt, "Eternal Life," *Chicago Studies* 48 (1965): 198–210; Werner Jaeger, "The Greek Ideas of Immortality," *Harvard Theological Review* 52 (1959): 135–47; J. K. Brandyberry, "Important Forgotten History: The Roots of Opposition to Resurrection Truth Among Today's Evangelical Leaders," *Resurrection* 94–95 (1991): 6–7; Theological Commission, "Some Current Questions in Eschatology," *Irish Theological Quarterly* 58 (1992): 209–43; B. L. Bateson, "The Resurrection of the Dead: 1 Corinthians 15:25," *Resurrection* 93 (1990): 5-6, 8; R. O. Zorn, "II Corinthians 5:1-10: Individual Eschatology or Corporate Solidarity, Which?" *Reformed Theological Review* 48 (1989): 93–104; R. S. Weathers, "Dualism or Holism? A Look at Biblical Anthropology, Ethics, and Human Health," *Journal of the American Scientific Affiliation* 35 (1983): 80–83.

8. C. J. De Vogel, "Reflections on Philipp. 1:23–24," *Novum Testamentum* 19 (1977): 262–74.

9. Plato, "Phaedo," in *Plato in Twelve Volumes, I. Euthyphro, Apology, Crito, Phaedo, Phaedrus,* trans. Harold N. Fowler (Cambridge: Harvard University Press, 1982): 193–404; Plato, *Plato: Lysis, Symposium, Gorgias,* trans. W. R. M. Lamb (Cambridge: Harvard University Press, 1925); and Plato, *The Republic of Plato,* trans. Allan Bloom (New York: HarperCollins, 1991); S. Jones, "Natural Immortality: Is It a Christian Doctrine?" *Resurrection* 95 (1992): 18–19.

10. Tertullian, *De Anima;* Gregory of Nyssa, "On the Making of Man," in *Select Writings and Letters of Gregory, Bishop of Nyssa,*

trans. Henry Austin Wilson, in *Nicene and Post-Nicene Fathers*, 2d series, ed. Philip Schaff and Henry Wace (Grand Rapids, Mich.: Eerdmans, 1988), vol. 5, 387–427; Gregory of Nyssa, "On the Soul and the Resurrection," in *Saint Gregory of Nyssa: Ascetical Works*, trans. Virginia W. Callahan (Washington, D.C.: Catholic University Press, 1967), 195–272; Augustine, *Confessions*; Augustine, "Immortality of the Soul," trans. Ludwig Schopp, in *The Fathers of the Church: Saint Augustine* (Washington, D.C.: Catholic University of America Press, 1984), 15–47; "The Magnitude of the Soul," trans. John J. McMahon, in *The Fathers of the Church: Saint Augustine* (Washington: Catholic University of America Press, 1984), 59–149; Augustine, *The Greatness of the Soul (De Quantitate Animae)*, trans. Joseph M. Colleran (Westminster, Md.: Newman Press, 1950); Augustine, "On the Soul and Its Origin," *Saint Augustine: Anti-Pelagian Writings* trans. Peter Holmes, Robert E. Wallis, and Benjamin B. Warfield, in *Nicene and Post-Nicene Fathers of the Christian Church*, first series, ed. Philip Schaff (Grand Rapids, Mich.: Eerdmans, 1991), vol. 5, 310–73; R. A. Markus, "Augustine," in *The Cambridge History of Later Greek and Early Medieval Philosophy*, ed. A. H. Armstrong (New York: Cambridge University Press, 1980), 341–61.

11. Oscar Cullmann, *Immortality of the Soul or Resurrection of the Dead?* (New York: Macmillan, 1958).

12. R. W. Brockway, "Immortality of the Soul: An Evangelical Heresy," *Religious Humanism* 13 (1979): 14–18; M. Bailey, "Biblical Man and Some Formulae of Christian Teaching," *Irish Theological Quarterly* 27 (1960): 173–200; H. V. White, "Immortality and Resurrection in Recent Theology," *Encounter* 22 (1961): 52–58.

13. Jaeger, "The Greek Ideas of Immortality," 135–47.

14. Edmond Jacob, "Psuche," in *Theological Dictionary of the New Testament*, ed. Gerhard Friedrich, trans. Geoffrey W. Bromiley (Grand Rapids, Mich.: Eerdmans, 1974), vol. 9, 631.

15. Berkouwer, *Man: The Image of God*, 194–233.

16. I. H. Marshall, "Uncomfortable Words, VI: 'Fear Him Who Can Destroy Both Soul and Body in Hell' (Mt. 10:28 RSV)," *Expository Times* 81 (1970): 276–82.

17. De Vogel, "Reflections on Philipp. 1:23–24," 262–74.

18. Heber F. Peackock, "Translating the Word for 'Soul' in the Old Testament," *Bible Translator* 27 (1976): 216–19.

19. Boyd, *Soul Psychology*, 5.

20. Niebuhr, *The Nature and Destiny of Man*, 5–13; Johannes Pedersen, *Israel: Its Life and Culture*, vol. 1 (London: Oxford University Press, 1926), 99–101; Rudolf Bultmann, "The Theology of

Paul," 191, 194–95, 204, 209; Purdy, "Paul the Apostle," 681–704; E. Earle Ellis, "Soma in First Corinthians," *Interpretation* 44 (1990): 132–44; and J. A. T. Robinson, *The Body: A Study in Pauline Theology* (Chicago: Regnery, 1952).

21. Hans Walter Wolff, *Anthropology of the Old Testament* (Philadelphia: Fortress Press, 1974); Freeman Barton, *Heaven, Hell and Hades* (Lenox, Mass: Henceforth, 1990), 13–80; John W. Cooper, *Body, Soul, and Life Everlasting: Biblical Anthropology and the Monism-Dualism Debate* (Grand Rapids, Mich.: Eerdmans, 1989).

22. Barr, *The Semantics of Biblical Language.*

23. James Barr, *The Garden of Eden and the Hope of Immortality* (London: SCM, 1992 and Minneapolis: Fortress Press, 1993).

24. Cooper, *Body, Soul, and Life Everlasting;* Cooper, "The Identity of Resurrected Persons: Fatal Flaws of Monistic Anthropology," *Calvin Theological Journal* 23 (1988): 19–36.

25. Millard J. Erickson, *Christian Theology* (Grand Rapids, Mich.: Baker Book House, 1994), 536–38.

26. Boyd, "One's Self-Concept and Biblical Theology."

27. Harry A. Wolfson, "Immortality and Resurrection in the Philosophy of the Church Fathers," in *Immortality and Resurrection,* ed. Krister Stendahl (New York: Macmillan, 1965), 54.

28. Cullmann wrote, "The lack of New Testament speculation about this does not give us the right simply to suppress the interim condition as such. I do not understand why Protestant theologians (including Barth) are so afraid of the New Testament position when the New Testament teaches only this much about the interim condition: (1) that it exists, (2) that it already signifies union with Christ." (See Cullmann, "Immortality of the Soul or Resurrection of the Dead?" in *Immortality and Resurrection,* 40, n. 34.)

29. Cooper, *Body, Soul, and Life Everlasting,* 1.

30. Joseph A. Komonchak, Mary Collins, and Dermot A. Lane, eds., *New Dictionary of Theology* (Collegeville, Minn.: Liturgical Press, 1987).

31. Thomas Aquinas, *Summa Theologica,* trans. Fathers of the English Dominican Province and Daniel J. Sullivan, in the series *Great Books of the Western World,* 54 vols. (Chicago: William Benton, Encyclopaedia Britannica, 1952), vol. 19, part 1, quest. 75–102; Aristotle, "On the Soul," in *Aristotle in Twenty-three Volumes, VIII, On the Soul, Parva Naturalia, On Breath,* trans. W. S. Hett (Cambridge: Harvard University Press, 1986), 2–203.

32. Heinrich Denzinger, Clemens Bannwart, and Johann B. Umberg, *Enchiridion Symbolorum* (Barcinone: Herder, 1957), 902.

33. Etienne Gilson, *Elements of Christian Philosophy* (New York: Doubleday, 1960), 228–29.

34. F. C. Copleston, *Aquinas: An Introduction to the Life and Work of the Great Medieval Thinker* (New York: Penguin Books, 1955), 169.

35. Mieczylaw A. Krapiec, "The Human Being in the Perspective of Death," in *I-Man*, trans. Marie Lescoe, Andrew Woznicki, Teresa Sandok et al. (New Britain, Conn.: Mariel Publications, 1983), 335f. See also Karl Rahner, *On the Meaning of Death* (New York: Herder & Herder, 1961); Johann Auer and Joseph Ratzinger, "The Immortality of the Soul and the Resurrection of the Dead," in *Dogmatic Theology, no. 9: Eschatology* (Washington, D.C.: Catholic University Press, 1988); and David Q. Liptak, letter of 22 August 1994 and conversation of 18 July 1995.

36. *Gaudium et Spes (Pastoral Constitution on the Church in the Modern World, Promulgated by His Holiness Pope Paul VI on December 7, 1965)*, translated by NCWC Translation (Boston: Saint Paul Editions, 1966).

37. *Catechism of the Catholic Church* (Liguori, Mo.: Liguori Publications, 1994), sec. 365, p. 93.

38. Ibid., 364. A footnote says that this quote comes from "*Gaudium et Spes* 14, ¶ 1."

39. Aquinas, *Summa Theologica*, part 1, quest. 75, art. 1.

40. Ibid., 75–102.

41. David Q. Liptak, letter of 22 August 1994 and conversation of July 18, 1994.

42. The classic Catholic discussion of the mental health movement is Francis J. Braceland, ed., *Faith, Reason, and Modern Psychiatry* (New York: P. J. Kenedy, 1955). That book, however, does not address the topic of this book, namely the relationship of the soul and secular psychology.

43. Gershon Winkler, *The Soul of the Matter*. The Kabbalah is a mystical trend in Judaism that is resurgent in recent years (Rabbi Eric Polokoff conversation of Oct. 31, 1995). Winkler writes, "While the soul, after death, is no longer manifested in the material realm of existence, it nevertheless remains operative on its original plane of existence, the spiritual realm. It is the body, therefore, which expires upon death, not the consciousness, as the Talmud illustrates. . . . Judaism does not view the relationship of the soul and the body as a union of conflict but rather as a union of cooperativeness. The body cannot function without the soul, nor can the soul fulfill itself without the body" (pp. 3, 6).

44. Marucice Lamm, *The Jewish Way in Death and Mourning* (New York: Jonathan David Publishers, 1969).

45. Simcha Paull Raphael, "Is There Afterlife after Auschwitz? Reflections on Life after Death in the 20th Century," *Judaism* 44 (1992): 346–60.

46. Dan Cohn-Sherbok, "Jewish Faith and the Holocaust," *Religious Studies* 26 (1990): 277–93; Cohn-Sherbok, "Death and Immortality in the Jewish Tradition," *Theology* 90 (1987): 263–73.

47. William Barrett, *Death of the Soul: From Descartes to the Computer* (New York: Doubleday, 1986).

48. Karl R. Popper and John C. Eccles, *The Self and Its Brain* (New York: Springer, 1977); and Cooper, *Body, Soul, and Life Everlasting*, 236–53.

49. Bennett, "Getting Used to Decadence."

50. Boyd, "Losing Soul"; Cooper, *Body, Soul, and Life Everlasting*; Cooper, "The Identity of Resurrected Persons," 19–36.

51. Jay E. Adams, *A Theology of Christian Counseling: More Than Redemption* (Grand Rapids, Mich.: Zondervan, 1979); John F. MacArthur Jr. and Wayne A. Mack, *Introduction to Biblical Counseling: A Basic Guide to the Principles and Practice of Counseling* (Dallas: Word Publishing, 1994).

52. Gallup Poll, *Religion in America, The Gallup Report #259*; Henry, Sims, and Spray, *The Fifth Profession*, 45–71.

53. American Psychiatric Association, "Guidelines Regarding Possible Conflict Between Psychiatrists' Religious Commitments and Psychiatric Practice," *American Journal of Psychiatry* 147 (1990): 542.

54. Albert Ellis, "Psychotherapy and Atheistic Values," 635–39.

55. Conversations with David Larson, 17 November 1992 and 28 February 1993. Quoted in Boyd, *Soul Psychology*, 73.

56. David Schiedermayer, *Putting the Soul Back in Medicine: Reflections on Compassion and Ethics* (Grand Rapids, Mich.: Baker Books, 1994).

57. "Patients' Spiritual Beliefs Need to Be Recognized in Psychiatric Treatment," *Psychiatric News* (17 March 1995): 9, 22.

58. Boyd, *Soul Psychology*, 183–84.

59. Robert Thomsen, *Bill W.* (New York: Harper & Row, 1985).

3. THE TRIUMPH OF THE THERAPEUTIC

1. Philip Rieff, *The Triumph of the Therapeutic: Uses of Faith After Freud* (Chicago: University of Chicago Press, 1987), 25.

2. Judith S. Wallerstein, "Children After Divorce: Wounds That Don't Heal," *New York Times Magazine,* 22 January 1989, 18–21, 41–44.

3. Walter Dorherty, *Soul Searching: Why Psychotherapy Must Promote Moral Responsibility* (New York: Basic Books, 1995); reviewed by Pepper Schwartz, "Parent and Child: When Staying Is Worth the Pain," *New York Times,* Connecticut section, 20 April 1995, C1, C4.

4. Cross-National Collaborative Group, "The Changing Rate of Major Depression: Cross-National Comparisons," *Journal of the American Medical Association* 268 (1992): 3098–3105; and Gerald L. Klerman and Myrna M. Weissman, "Increasing Rates of Depression," *Journal of the American Medical Association* 261 (1989): 2229–35.

5. Paul C. Vitz, *Psychology as Religion: The Cult of Self Worship* (Grand Rapids, Mich.: Eerdmans, 1994).

6. Ibid., 19.

7. Ibid., xii.

8. Boyd, *Affirming the Soul,* 156.

9. George Johnston, "Spirit," in *Theological Word Book of the Bible,* ed. Alan Richardson (New York: Macmillan, 1950), 234.

10. Wells, *No Place for Truth.*

11. Rick Matson and Sarah Smith, conversation of September 12, 1995.

12. Karl Menninger, *What Ever Happened to Sin?* (New York: Bantam, 1988).

13. Bettelheim, *Freud and Man's Soul,* 74; and Bettelheim, "Reflections: Freud and the Soul," *New Yorker,* 1 March 1982, 52–93, especially 86.

14. Sigmund Freud, *"Psychische Behandlung (Seelenbehandlung)"* ["Treatment of the *Psyche* (Treatment of the Soul)"], in *Die Gesundheit,* ed. R. Kossmann and J. Weiss (Stuttgart, Berlin, and Leipzig: Union Deutsche Verlagsgesellschaft, 1905), vol. 1, 368–84. Translation is by Jeffrey H. Boyd; see *Soul Psychology,* 336–37, n. 77. Bettelheim offers a similar translation in "Reflections: Freud and Man's Soul."

15. Ernest Jones, *The Life and Work of Sigmund Freud,* vol. 2 (New York: Basic Books, 1960), 421.

16. Boyd, "Losing Soul" and "One's Self-Concept."

4. THE ALLEGEDLY HOLISTIC, UNIFIED PERSON

1. In order to understand what U.S. culture is teaching us about ourselves, I went to a leading source: *Self* magazine, which is sold at virtually every grocery store and pharmacy. The January 1995 issue revealed that the target audience was young women, and women who wish they were still young. The photographs showed smiling women with incredibly fit bodies, none above the age of twenty-five. The articles emphasized these subjects: trim another inch off your tummy, eat right, exercise aerobically, have ageless skin, dress to look sexy, be enthusiastic, and thereby win at the game of life. Certain subjects were never mentioned: God, ethics, morality, death, old age, or values such as self-denial or loving your enemies. The word "guilt" was mentioned only once, in an article written by the editor, Alexandra Penney. She wrote one page about how the magazine had helped her to live a healthier life. Before she became editor, she had "been living a high-fat, mega-sugar, caffeine-brimmed, slothful life," and "didn't even feel guilty about it." The use of "guilty" here does not refer to any assault against God, or to any exploitation of one's neighbor, but to failure to take good care of one's body.

Thus the January 1995 issue of *Self* appeared to promote the gospel of self-esteem as the best way to find fulfillment in life. It never discussed the problem Jesus mentioned: she who seeks her life will lose it (Matt. 16:25; Mark 8:35; Luke 9:24, 17:33; John 12:25). Jesus taught that the self can be found only through self-sacrificial love of God and neighbor. It cannot be found or fulfilled directly.

2. Cooper, *Body, Soul, and Life Everlasting;* Cooper, "The Identity of Resurrected Persons," 19–36.

3. A popular book on this is Walter Pierpaoli, William Regelson, and Carol Colman, *The Melatonin Miracle: Nature's Age-Reversing, Disease-Fighting, Sex-Enhancing Hormone* (New York: Simon & Schuster, 1995).

4. Caroline Bynum, *Resurrection of the Body,* xviii.

5. In the pseudepigraphic tradition it is said that Moses was "taken away" by God, without tasting death (*Assumption of Moses* 11:9f; Edmond Jacob, "Immortality," in *Interpreter's Dictionary of the Bible,* vol. 2, 689; Barr, *Garden of Eden,* 15–16.) This may well be why Moses and Elijah met with Jesus at the Transfiguration in the Synoptic Gospels, because they were immortal men, like Jesus.

The same theme is found in the following verse about the end of the world: "And they shall see those who were taken up, who from their birth have not tasted death" (2 Esdr. 6:26). The term "taken up" refers to those who were taken directly to Heaven without dying. Ezra also was said to have been "taken up" (2 Esdr. 8:19): "For you [Ezra] shall be taken up from among humankind, and henceforth you shall live with my Son and with those who are like you, until the times are ended" (2 Esdr. 14:9).

6. Murray J. Harris, *From Grave to Glory: Resurrection in the New Testament, Including a Response to Norman L. Geisler* (Grand Rapids, Mich.: Zondervan, 1990); and Harris, *Raised Immortal: Resurrection and Immortality in the New Testament* (Grand Rapids, Mich.: Eerdmans, 1985). See T. C. Morgan, "The Mother of All Muddles: Evangelical Theologians Clash in Public over What Kind of Body Jesus Christ Has Following His Resurrection," *Christianity Today* (5 April 1993): 62–66; and Norman L. Geisler, "A Response to Murray Harris," in *Battle for Resurrection* (Nashville: Thomas Nelson, 1992), 174–202.

7. Oscar Cullmann, "Immortality of the Soul or Resurrection of the Dead?" in *Immortality and Resurrection,* ed. Krister Stendahl (New York: Macmillan, 1965), 40, n. 34. See also J. Osei-Bonsu, "The Intermediate State in the New Testament," *Scottish Journal of Theology* 44 (1991): 169–94.

8. N. S. L. Fryer, "The Intermediate State in Paul," *Hervormde Teologiese Stud* 43 (1987): 448–84; J. Osei-Bonsu, "The Intermediate State in the New Testament," 169–94; D. Moody, "The Double Face of Death," *Review and Expositor* 58 (1961): 348–66.

9. Boyd, "One's Self-Concept and Biblical Theology."

10. John W. Cooper, "The Identity of Resurrected Persons," 19–36.

11. Augustine, "The Magnitude of the Soul" and "The Immortality of the Soul."

12. Robert M. Post, "Transduction of Psychosocial Stress into the Neurobiology of Recurrent Affective Disorder," *American Journal of Psychiatry* 149 (1992): 999–1010; Post and S. R. B. Weiss, "The Neurobiology of Treatment-Resistant Mood Disorders," in *Psychopharmacology: The Fourth Generation of Progress,* ed. F. E. Bloom and D. J. Kupfer (New York: Raven Press, 1995), 1155–70; M. Clark, R. M. Post, S. R. Weiss, and T. Nakajima, "Expression of C-fos mRNA in Acute and Kindled Cocaine Seizures in Rats," *Brain Research* 582 (1992): 101–6.

13. D. G. Jones, "The Relationship between the Brain and the

Mind," *Journal of the American Scientific Affiliation* 33 (1981): 193–202; G. R. Gillet, "Brain, Mind, and Soul," *Zygon* 20 (1985): 425–34.

14. Wilder Penfield, *The Mystery of the Mind* (Princeton, N.J.: Princeton University Press, 1975), 113–14.

15. Popper and Eccles, *The Self and Its Brain*, 11.

16. N. Rosenthal, "Molecular Medicine: Regulation of Gene Expression," *New England Journal of Medicine* 331 (6 October 1994): 931–33; R. L. Margolis, D. M. Chuang, and R. M. Post, "Programmed Cell Death: Implications for Neuropsychiatric Disorders," *Biological Psychiatry* 35 (15 June 1994): 946–56.

17. Leander Keck phone conversation, November 12, 1993.

5. Defining—and Redefining—the Soul

1. Catherine Kroeger telephone interview, April 20, 1994.

2. Eduard Schweizer, "New Testament Usage [of *Psyche*] in Distinction from *Pneuma*," *Theological Dictionary of the New Testament*, ed. Gerhard Friedrich, trans. Geoffrey W. Bromiley (Grand Rapids, Mich.: Eerdmans, 1974), vol. 9, 654–55.

3. Ibid.

4. *Psychikos* "always denoted the life of the natural world and whatever belongs to it, in contrast to the supernatural world, which is characterized by *pneuma*." William F. Arndt and F. Wilbur Gingrich, *A Greek-English Lexicon of the New Testament and Other Early Christian Literature* (Chicago: University of Chicago Press, 1979), 894.

5. Boyd, "Losing Soul."

6. Peackock, "Translating the Word for 'Soul,'" 216–19.

7. Edward W. Goodrick and John R. Kohlenberger III, *The NIV Exhaustive Concordance* (Grand Rapids, Mich.: Zondervan, 1990), 1546–47, 1808. This issue cannot be easily studied in the New Revised Standard Version, because its Concordance lacks an appendix that lists each separate Hebrew and Greek word.

8. Johannes Pedersen, *Israel*.

9. Plotinus, "Fourth Ennead (On the Soul)," in *Plotinus, the Six Enneads*, trans. Stephen MacKenna and B. S. Page, in the series *Great Books of the Western World*, 54 vols. (Chicago: William Benton, Encyclopaedia Britannica, 1952), vol. 17, 139–207; A. H. Armstrong, "Plotinus," in *The Cambridge History of Later Greek and Early Medieval Philosophy*, ed. A. H. Armstrong (New York: Cambridge University Press, 1980), 195–271.

10. Berkouwer, *Man: The Image of God;* A. Hoekema, *Created in God's Image* (Grand Rapids, Mich.: Eerdmans, 1986).

11. Aquinas, *Summa Theologica,* part 1, quest. 75–102; *Catechism of the Catholic Church,* sec. 364–65, p. 93; Aristotle, "On the Soul," 2–203.

12. John W. Cooper, conversation of 18 July 1995.

13. Frank J. Sheed, *Theology for Beginners* (Ann Arbor, Mich.: Servant, 1982); Liptak, conversation of 19 July 1995; Krapiec, "The Human Being in the Perspective of Death," 335–62.

14. Aquinas, *Summa Theologica,* part 1, quest. 75, art. 1.

15. D. A. Shewmon, "The Metaphysics of Brain Death, Persistent Vegetative State, and Dementia," *Thomist* 49 (1985): 24–80; Ph. Smith, "Brain Death: A Thomistic Appraisal," *Angelicum* 67 (1990): 3–36.

16. Liptak, conversation of 19 July 1995; Sheed, *Theology for Beginners.*

17. Heinz Kohut, *How Does Analysis Cure?,* ed. Arnold Goldberg and Paul Stepansky (Chicago: University of Chicago Press, 1984); Kohut, *The Restoration of the Self* (Madison, Conn.: International Universities Press, 1990); Kohut, *Self Psychology and the Humanities,* ed. Charles B. Strozier (New York: W. W. Norton, 1985); Ernest S. Wolf, *Treating the Self: Elements of Clinical Self Psychology* (New York: Guilford Press, 1988).

18. Ernest White, *Christian Life and the Unconscious* (New York: Harper & Brothers, 1955).

19. Gordon R. Lewis and Bruce A. Demarest, *Integrative Theology,* vol. 3 (Grand Rapids, Mich.: Zondervan, 1994), 17–240.

20. Adams, *A Theology of Christian Counseling.*

6. THE SOUL AS SOURCE OF HUMOR AND WIT

1. Joseph Addison, "Cato," act 5, scene 1, in *Bartlett's Familiar Quotations.*

2. Cullmann, *Immortality of the Soul or Resurrection of the Dead?;* see also Cullman, "Immortality or Resurrection?" *Christianity Today* 2.21 (21 July 1958): 6; and Cullman, "Immortality of the Soul or Resurrection of the Dead?" in *Immortality and Resurrection.*

3. Jaeger, "The Greek Ideas," 135–47.

4. Niebuhr, *The Nature and Destiny of Man,* 5–13; Pedersen, *Israel,* 99–101; Bultmann, "The Theology of Paul," 191, 194–95, 204,

209; Purdy, "Paul the Apostle," 681–704; E. Earle Ellis, "Soma in First Corinthians," 132–44; and Robinson, *The Body*.

5. Moore, *Care of the Soul*.

CONCLUSION

1. George H. Gallup Jr., "Empowering the Laity," in *Yearbook of American and Canadian Churches 1993,* ed. Kenneth B. Bedell (Nashville: Abingdon Press, 1993), 17–18.

2. C. Kirk Hadaway, *Church Growth Principles: Separating Fact from Fiction* (Nashville: Broadman Press, 1991).

3. Data in Table 3 are from Loren B. Mead, *Transforming Congregations for the Future* (Washington, D.C.: Alban Institute, 1994), 128. Similarly, the Gallup Poll finds that between 1967 and 1986 the percentage of Americans in mainline denominations fell as follows: Methodists, 14 percent (of the U.S. population) to 9 percent; Lutherans, 7 percent to 5 percent; Presbyterians, 6 percent to 2 percent; Episcopalians, 3 percent to 2 percent. UCC is not listed in that study. In that same time span the Baptists (predominantly Southern Baptists) held their own, from 21 percent to 20 percent. Catholics grew slightly, from 25 percent to 27 percent. (Gallup Poll, *Religion in America: The Gallup Report* #259, April 1987, 18–19.)

4. For information on Episcopal church growth, see Kirk Hadaway, "The Decline Continues: An Analysis of Membership Trends in the United Church of Christ," report by the United Church Board for Homeland Ministries (Cleveland: UCBHM, 1995), p. 5.

5. Many people have alternative theories to explain the loss of parishioners. For example, a recent study in the United Methodist church cited the following theory for the decline: Methodism "has become middle-class and is in decline in large measure because of its lack of outreach to all sorts and conditions of persons. We have opted for a very narrow sociological group for our ministry and mission. There will be no recovery from decline unless we recover Wesley's missionary impulse to reach out and welcome all." (The Association of United Methodist Theological Schools, *Agenda 21: United Methodist Ministry for a New Century,* National Report, October 1995, 28.)

6. New International, New Revised Standard, Revised Standard, New Jerusalem, Jerusalem, New King James, New American Standard, New American, New English, Revised English, Anchor, New Oxford Annotated, Reader's Digest, The Complete, The Am-

plified, The Living Bible, The Good News Bible, James Moffatt's translation, and *The Torah,* from the Jewish Publication Society.

7. Thomas Kuhn, *The Structure of Scientific Revolutions* (Chicago: University of Chicago Press, 1971); cited in Van Leeuwen, *The Person in Psychology,* 7.

8. Michael D. Lemonick, "Glimpses of the Mind: What Is Consciousness? Memory? Emotions? Science Unravels the Best-Kept Secrets of the Human Brain," *Time,* 17 July 1995, 44–52.

9. E. Fuller Torrey, *Freudian Fraud: The Malignant Effect of Freud's Theory on American Thought and Culture* (New York: HarperCollins, 1992).

10. James Barr, conversation with author, November 22, 1993.

11. For a classic text from this perspective, see Franz Delitzsch, *A System of Biblical Psychology,* trans. Robert E. Wallis (Grand Rapids, Mich.: Baker Book House, 1966).

12. Conversation with Benoit Mandelbrot, October 28, 1991.

13. James Gleick, *Chaos: Making of a New Science* (New York: Penguin Books, 1988); Edward Lorenz, "Deterministic Nonperiodic Flow," *Journal of Atmospheric Sciences* 20 (1963): 130–41; and Lorenz, "On the Prevalence of Aperiodicity in Simple Systems," in *Global Analysis,* ed. Miroslav Grmela and Jerrold E. Marsden (New York: Springer-Verlag, 1979), 53–75.

14. The National Council of Churches finds that "denominations that are very visible in the public media like the Presbyterian Church (U.S.A.), the Episcopal Church, and the United Church of Christ are not even in the top seven largest denominations." They find that Pentecostal denominations, such as the Assemblies of God and the Church of God in Christ, were the fastest-growing denominations in the United States in the 1980s. The latter is now the fifth-largest denomination in the U.S. (Bedell, "Introduction," in *Yearbook of American and Canadian Churches, 1993*).

The Southern Baptist Convention has grown to be the largest U.S. Protestant denomination, with 17 million members (Barry A. Kosmin and Seymour P. Lachman, *One Nation Under God: Religion in Contemporary American Society* (New York: Harmony Books, 1993), 39, 52).

15. Boyd, *Soul Psychology,* 267–70. Leslie Dickerson was not and is not a patient of mine. This is her real name, however; she asked that I not use a pseudonym.

BIBLIOGRAPHY

Adams, Jay E. *A Theology of Christian Counseling: More Than Redemption*. Grand Rapids, Mich.: Zondervan, 1979.

American Psychiatric Association. "Guidelines Regarding Possible Conflict between Psychiatrists' Religious Commitments and Psychiatric Practice." *American Journal of Psychiatry* 147 (1990): 542.

American Psychiatric Association Task Force Report 10: Psychiatrists' Viewpoints on Religion and Their Services to Religious Institutions and the Ministry. Washington, D.C.: American Psychiatric Association, 1975.

Aquinas, Thomas. *Summa Theologica*. Translated by the Fathers of the English Dominican Province and Daniel J. Sullivan. Vol. 19 in the series *Great Books of the Western World*. 54 vols. Chicago: William Benton, Encyclopaedia Britannica, 1952.

Aristotle. "On the Soul." In *Aristotle in Twenty-three Volumes: Vol. VIII—On the Soul, Parva Naturalia, On Breath*, translated by W. S. Hett, 2–203. Cambridge: Harvard University Press, 1986.

Armstrong, A. H. "Plotinus." In *The Cambridge History of Later Greek and Early Medieval Philosophy*, edited by A. H. Armstrong, 195–271. New York: Cambridge University Press, 1980.

Arndt, William F., and F. Wilbur Gingrich. *A Greek-English Lexicon of the New Testament and Other Early Christian Literature*. Chicago: University of Chicago Press, 1979.

Association of United Methodist Theological Schools, *Agenda 21: United Methodist Ministry for a New Century,* National Report, October 1995, n.p.

Auer, Johann, and Joseph Ratzinger. "The Immortality of the Soul and the Resurrection of the Dead." In *Dogmatic Theology, no. 9: Eschatology.* Washington, D.C.: Catholic University Press, 1988.

Augustine. *Confessions.* Translated by R. S. Pine-Coffin. New York: Penguin Books, 1987.

———. *The Greatness of the Soul (De Quantitate Animae).* Translated by Joseph M. Colleran. Westminster, Md.: Newman Press, 1950.

———. "Immortality of the Soul," translated by Ludwig Schopp. In *The Fathers of the Church: Saint Augustine,* 15–47. Washington, D.C.: Catholic University of America Press, 1984.

———. "The Magnitude of the Soul," translated by John J. McMahon. In *The Fathers of the Church: Saint Augustine,* 59–149. Washington, D.C.: Catholic University of America Press, 1984.

———. "On the Soul and Its Origin." In *Saint Augustine: Anti-Pelagian Writings,* translated by Peter Holmes, Robert E. Wallis, and Benjamin B. Warfield. In *Nicene and Post-Nicene Fathers of the Christian Church,* first series, vol. 5, edited by Philip Schaff, 310–73. Grand Rapids, Mich.: Eerdmans, 1991.

Bailey, M. "Biblical Man and Some Formulae of Christian Teaching." *Irish Theological Quarterly* 27 (1960): 173–200.

Barr, James. *The Garden of Eden and the Hope of Immortality.* London: SCM, 1992; Minneapolis: Fortress Press, 1993.

———. *The Semantics of Biblical Language.* Philadelphia: Trinity Press International, 1961.

Barrett, William. *Death of the Soul: From Descartes to the Computer.* New York: Doubleday, 1986.

Barth, Karl. *Church Dogmatics.* Edited by G. W. Bromiley and T. F. Torrance. Translated by H. Knight, G. W. Bromiley, J. K. S. Reid, and R. H. Fuller. Edinburgh: T. & T. Clark Publishers, 1960.

Barton, Freeman. *Heaven, Hell, and Hades.* Lenox, Mass: Henceforth, 1990.

Bateson, B. L. "The Resurrection of the Dead: 1 Corinthians 15:25." *Resurrection* 93 (1990): 5–6, 8.

Bedell, Kenneth B., ed. *Yearbook of American and Canadian Churches, 1993.* Nashville: Abingdon Press, 1993.

Bennett, William J. "Getting Used to Decadence: The Spirit of Democracy in Modern America." *Heritage Lectures* #477 (December 1993). Heritage Foundation, Washington, D.C.

Berkouwer, C. G. *Man: The Image of God.* Grand Rapids, Mich.: Eerdmans, 1962.

Bettelheim, Bruno. *Freud and Man's Soul.* New York: Random House, 1984.

———. "Reflections: Freud and the Soul." *New Yorker,* 1 March 1982, 52–93.

Bloomqist, Wayne, ed. *Soul and Its Powers.* Wilmot, Wis.: Lotus Light, 1992.

Boyd, Jeffrey H. *Affirming the Soul: Remarkable Conversations between Mental Health Professionals and an Ordained Minister.* Cheshire, Conn.: Soul Research Institute, 1994.

———. "Apocalypse from Nuclear War Compared with the Expected Apocalypse of October 22, 1844." *Henceforth* (spring 1996).

———. "Losing Soul: How and Why Theologians Created the Mental Health Movement." *Calvin Theological Journal* 30 (November 1995): 472–92.

———. "Mental Health Professionals and 'the Soul.'" *Journal of Psychology and Theology* 23 (fall 1995): 151–60.

———. "On Use of the Term 'Soul.'" *Journal of Psychology and Theology* 23 (fall 1995): 161–70.

———. "One's Self-Concept and Biblical Theology." *Journal of the Evangelical Theological Society,* in press.

———. *Soul Psychology: How to Understand Your Soul in Light of the Mental Health Movement.* Cheshire, Conn.: Soul Research Institute, 1994.

Braceland, Francis J., ed. *Faith, Reason, and Modern Psychiatry.* New York: P. J. Kenedy, 1955.

Brandyberry, J. K. "Important Forgotten History: The Roots of Opposition to Resurrection Truth among Today's Evangelical Leaders." *Resurrection* 94–95 (1991): 6–7.

Brockway, R. W. "Immortality of the Soul: An Evangelical Heresy." *Religious Humanism* 13 (1979): 14–18.

Brothers, Leslie. "A Biological Perspective on Empathy." *American Journal of Psychiatry* 146 (1989): 10–19.

Bultmann, Rudolf. "The Theology of Paul." In *Theology of the New Testament,* vol. 1, translated by Kendrick Grobel. London: SCM Press, 1965.

Bynum, Caroline W. *The Resurrection of the Body in Western Christianity, 200–1336.* New York: Columbia University Press, 1995.

Catechism of the Catholic Church. Liguori, Mo.: Liguori Publications, 1994.

Chomsky, Noam. *Syntactic Structures.* The Hague: Mouton, 1957.

Clark, M., R. M. Post, S. R. Weiss, and T. Nakajima. "Expression of C-fos mRNA in Acute and Kindled Cocaine Seizures in Rats." *Brain Research* 582 (1992): 101–6.

Cohn-Sherbok, Dan. "Death and Immortality in the Jewish Tradition." *Theology* 90 (1987): 263–73.

———. "Jewish Faith and the Holocaust." *Religious Studies* 26 (1990): 277–93.

Collins, Kenneth J. *Soul Care: Deliverance and Renewal through the Christian Life.* Wheaton, Ill.: Victor Books, 1995.

Cooper, John W. *Body, Soul, and Life Everlasting: Biblical Anthropology and the Monism-Dualism Debate.* Grand Rapids, Mich.: Eerdmans, 1989.

———. "The Identity of Resurrected Persons: Fatal Flaws of Monistic Anthropology." *Calvin Theological Journal* 23 (1988): 19–36.

Copleston, F. C. *Aquinas: An Introduction to the Life and Work of the Great Medieval Thinker.* New York: Penguin Books, 1955.

Cousineau, Phil, ed. *Soul of the World: A Modern Book of Hours.* San Francisco: HarperSanFrancisco, 1993.

Covey, Stephen R., A. Roger Merrill, and Rebecca R. Merrill. *First Things First*. New York: Simon & Schuster, 1994.

Cross-National Collaborative Group. "The Changing Rate of Major Depression: Cross-National Comparisons." *Journal of the American Medical Association* 268 (1992): 3098–3105.

Cullmann, Oscar. *Immortality of the Soul or Resurrection of the Dead?* New York: Macmillan and Co., 1958.

———. "Immortality or Resurrection?" *Christianity Today* 2, no. 21 (21 July 1958): 6.

Day, Thomas. *Where Have You Gone, Michelangelo? The Loss of Soul in Catholic Culture*. New York: Crossroad, 1993.

———. *Why Catholics Can't Sing: The Culture of Catholicism and the Triumph of Bad Taste*. New York: Crossroad, 1990.

Delitzsch, Franz. *A System of Biblical Psychology*. Translated by Robert E. Wallis. Grand Rapids, Mich.: Baker Book House, 1966.

Denzinger, Heinrich, Clemens Bannwart, and Johann B. Umberg. *Enchiridion Symbolorum*. Barcinone: Herder, 1957.

De Vogel, C. J. "Reflections on Philipp. 1:23–24." *Novum Testamentum* 19 (1977): 262–74.

Dorherty, Walter. *Soul Searching: Why Psychotherapy Must Promote Moral Responsibility*. New York: Basic Books, 1995.

Edelman, Marian Wright. *The Measure of Our Success: A Letter to My Children and Yours*. Boston: Beacon Press, 1992.

Ellis, Albert. "Psychotherapy and Atheistic Values: A Response to A. Bergin's 'Psychotherapy and Religious Values.'" *Journal of Consulting and Clinical Psychology* 48 (1980): 635–39.

Ellis, E. Earle. "Sōma in First Corinthians." *Interpretation* 44 (1990): 132–44.

Erickson, Millard J. *Christian Theology*. Grand Rapids, Mich.: Baker Book House, 1994.

Fink, P. J. "Psychiatrists' Role in Managed Care Programs." *Hospital and Community Psychiatry* 44 (1993): 723–24.

Freud, Sigmund. "Civilization and Its Discontents." In *The Standard Edition of the Complete Psychological Works of Sig-*

mund Freud, vol. 21, translated by James Strachey, 64–145. London: Hogarth Press, 1986.

———. *"Psychische Behandlung (Seelenbehandlung)."* In *Die Gesundheit,* vol. 1, edited by R. Kossmann and J. Weiss, 368–84. Stuttgart, Berlin, and Leipzig: Union Deutsche Verlagsgesellschaft, 1905.

Fryer, N. S. L. "The Intermediate State in Paul." *Hervormde Teologiese Stud* 43 (1987): 448–84.

Gaddy, C. Welton. *Soul Under Siege: Surviving Clergy Depression.* Louisville, Ky.: Westminster John Knox, 1991.

Gallup, George H., Jr. "Empowering the Laity." In *Yearbook of American and Canadian Churches 1993,* edited by Kenneth B. Bedell, 17–18. Nashville: Abingdon Press, 1993.

Gallup Poll. *Religion in America: The Gallup Report #259,* April 1987.

Gaudium et Spes (Pastoral Constitution on the Church in the Modern World, Promulgated by His Holiness Pope Paul VI on December 7, 1965). Translated by NCWC Translation. Boston: Saint Paul Editions, 1966.

Geisler, Norman L. *Battle for Resurrection.* Nashville: Thomas Nelson, 1992.

Gillet, G. R. "Brain, Mind, and Soul." *Zygon* 20 (1985): 425–34.

Gilson, Etienne. *Elements of Christian Philosophy.* New York: Doubleday, 1960.

Gleick, James. *Chaos: Making of a New Science.* New York: Penguin Books, 1988.

Goodrick, Edward W., and John R. Kohlenberger III. *The NIV Exhaustive Concordance.* Grand Rapids, Mich.: Zondervan, 1990.

Gregory of Nyssa. "On the Making of Man." In *Select Writings and Letters of Gregory, Bishop of Nyssa,* translated by Henry Austin Wilson. In *Nicene and Post-Nicene Fathers,* second series, vol. 5, edited by Philip Schaff and Henry Wace, 387–427. Grand Rapids, Mich.: Eerdmans, 1988.

———. "On the Soul and the Resurrection." In *Saint Gregory of Nyssa: Ascetical Works,* translated by Virginia W. Callahan, 195–272. Washington, D.C.: Catholic University Press, 1967.

Grosso, Michael. *Soul Maker: Stories from the Far Side of the Psyche*. Norfolk, Va.: Hampton Roads Publishing Co., 1991.

Hadaway, C. Kirk. *Church Growth Principles: Separating Fact from Fiction*. Nashville: Broadman Press, 1991.

Harris, Murray J. *From Grave to Glory: Resurrection in the New Testament, Including a Response to Norman L. Geisler*. Grand Rapids, Mich.: Zondervan, 1990.

———. *Raised Immortal: Resurrection and Immortality in the New Testament*. Grand Rapids, Mich.: Eerdmans, 1985.

Heick, O. W. "If a Man Die, Shall He Live Again?" *Lutheran Quarterly* 17 (1965): 99–110.

Henry, W. E., J. H. Sims, and S. L. Spray. *The Fifth Profession*. San Francisco: Jossey-Bass, 1971.

Hillman, James. *Anima: An Anatomy of a Personified Notion*. Dallas: Spring Publications, 1985.

———. *Archetypal Psychology: A Brief Account*. Dallas: Spring Publications, 1983.

———. *The Dream and the Underworld*. New York: HarperCollins, 1979.

———. *Emotion: A Comprehensive Phenomenology of Theories and Their Meanings for Therapies*. Evanston, Ill.: Northwestern University Press, 1992.

———. *Healing Fiction*. Barrytown, N.Y.: Station Hill Press, 1983.

———. *Insearch: Psychology and Religion*. Dallas: Spring Publications, 1967.

———. *Kinds of Power: An Intelligent Guide to Its Uses*. New York: Doubleday, 1995.

———. *The Myth of Analysis*. New York: HarperCollins, 1992.

———. *Revisioning Psychology*. New York: HarperCollins, 1992.

———. *Suicide and the Soul*. Dallas: Spring Publications, 1964.

———. *The Thought of the Heart and the Soul of the World*. Dallas: Spring Publications, 1992.

Hillman, James, and Michael Ventura. *We've Had a Hundred Years of Psychotherapy—and the World's Getting Worse*. San Francisco: HarperSanFrancisco, 1992.

Hoekema, A. *Created in God's Image*. Grand Rapids, Mich.: Eerdmans, 1986.

Hopson, Darlene P. *Soul Mates*. New York: Prentice Hall, 1992.

Ingerman, Sandra. *Soul Retrieval: Mending the Fragmented Self through Shamanic Practice*. San Francisco: HarperSanFrancisco, 1991.

Jacob, Edmund. "Immortality." In *Interpreter's Dictionary of the Bible: An Illustrated Encyclopedia*. 4 vols. plus supplement. Vol. 2, edited by Charles A. Buttrick, Thomas S. Kepler, John Knox, Herbert G. May, Samuel Terrien, and Emory S. Bucke, 689–90. Nashville: Abingdon Press, 1981.

———. "Psyche." In *Theological Dictionary of the New Testament*, vol. 9, edited by Gerhard Friedrich, translated by Geoffrey W. Bromiley, 631. Grand Rapids, Mich.: Eerdmans, 1974.

Jaeger, Werner. "The Greek Ideas of Immortality." *Harvard Theological Review* 52 (1959): 135–47.

Jellinek, M. S., and B. Nurcombe. "Two Wrongs Don't Make a Right: Managed Care, Mental Health, and the Marketplace." *Journal of the American Medical Association* 270 (1993): 1737–39.

Johnston, George. "Spirit." In *Theological Word Book of the Bible*, edited by Alan Richardson, 233–47. New York: Macmillan, 1950.

Johnstone, Charlotte. "It's Easier to Wear Fruit on Your Head Than to Feed It to a Baby." *Family Circle*, 14 March 1995, 121.

Jones, D. G. "The Relationship between the Brain and the Mind." *Journal of the American Scientific Affiliation* 33 (1981): 193–202.

Jones, Ernest. *The Life and Work of Sigmund Freud*. 3 vols. New York: Basic Books, 1960.

Jones, S. "Natural Immortality: Is It a Christian Doctrine?" *Resurrection* 95 (1992): 18–19.

Jung, Carl G. *Modern Man in Search of a Soul*. Translated by W. S. Bell and Cary F. Baynes. New York: Harcourt Brace Jovanovich, 1933.

———. *On the Nature of the Psyche*. Translated by R. F. C. Hull. Princeton, N.J.: Princeton University Press, 1960.

Kelsey, Morton T. *Encounter with God.* Minneapolis: Bethany Fellowship, 1972.

Kendler, Kenneth S. "Overview: A Current Perspective on Twin Studies of Schizophrenia." *American Journal of Psychiatry* 140 (1983): 1413–25.

Klerman, Gerald L., and Myrna M. Weissman. "Increasing Rates of Depression." *Journal of the American Medical Association* 261 (1989): 2229–35.

Kohut, Heinz. *How Does Analysis Cure?* Edited by Arnold Goldberg and Paul Stepansky. Chicago: University of Chicago Press, 1984.

———. *The Restoration of the Self.* Madison, Conn.: International Universities Press, 1990.

———. *Self Psychology and the Humanities.* Edited by Charles B. Strozier. New York: W. W. Norton, 1985.

Komonchak, Joseph A., Mary Collins, and Dermot A. Lane, eds. *New Dictionary of Theology.* Collegeville, Minn.: Liturgical Press, 1987.

Kormin, Barry A., and Seymour P. Lachman. *One Nation Under God: Religion in Contemporary American Society.* New York: Harmony Books, 1993.

Krapiec, Mieczylaw A. "The Human Being in the Perspective of Death." In *I-Man,* translated by Marie Lescoe, Andrew Woznicki, Teresa Sandok et al. New Britain, Conn.: Mariel Publications, 1983.

Kuhn, Thomas. *The Structure of Scientific Revolutions.* Chicago: University of Chicago Press, 1971.

Kushner, Harold S. *When Bad Things Happen to Good People.* New York: Avon Publishers, 1983.

Lamm, Marucice. *The Jewish Way in Death and Mourning.* New York: Jonathan David Publishers, 1969.

Lancer, Bob. *Soulmate Process.* Malibu, Calif.: Valley Sun, 1992.

Larson, David B., E. Mansell Pattison, Dan G. Blazer, Abdul R. Omran, and Berton H. Kaplan. "Systematic Analysis of Research on Religious Variables in Four Major Psychiatric Journals 1978–1982." *American Journal of Psychiatry* 143 (1986): 329–34.

Lazarus, A. "Ten Reasons Why Psychiatrists May Dislike Managed Competition." *Hospital and Community Psychiatry* 45 (1994): 496–98.

Leech, Kenneth. *Soul Friend: An Invitation to Spiritual Direction.* San Francisco: HarperSanFrancisco, 1992.

Lemonick, Michael D. "Glimpses of the Mind: What Is Consciousness? Memory? Emotions? Science Unravels the Best-Kept Secrets of the Human Brain." *Time,* 17 July 1995, 44–52.

Lewis, Gordon R., and Bruce A. Demarest. *Integrative Theology,* vols. 2 and 3. Grand Rapids, Mich.: Zondervan, 1990, 1994.

Lindhardt, P. G. "Eternal Life." *Chicago Studies* 48 (1965): 198–210.

Liptak, David Q. "The Mind of John Paul II (Book Review)." *Homiletic and Pastoral Review* (February 1994): 76–77.

Lodge, David. *Souls and Bodies.* New York: Viking Penguin, 1990.

Lord, Peter. *Soul Care.* Grand Rapids, Mich.: Baker Books, 1990.

Lorenz, Edward. "Deterministic Nonperiodic Flow." *Journal of Atmospheric Sciences* 20 (1963): 130–41.

———. "On the Prevalence of Aperiodicity in Simple Systems." In *Global Analysis,* edited by Miroslav Grmela and Jerrold E. Marsden, 53–75. New York: Springer-Verlag, 1979.

MacArthur, John F., Jr., and Wayne A. Mack. *Introduction to Biblical Counseling: A Basic Guide to the Principles and Practice of Counseling.* Dallas: Word Publishing, 1994.

Margolis, R. L., D. M. Chuang, and R. M. Post. "Programmed Cell Death: Implications for Neuropsychiatric Disorders." *Biological Psychiatry* 35 (15 June 1994): 946–56.

Markus, R. A. "Augustine." In *The Cambridge History of Later Greek and Early Medieval Philosophy,* edited by A. H. Armstrong, 341–61. New York: Cambridge University Press, 1980.

Marshall, I. H. "Uncomfortable Words, VI: 'Fear Him Who Can Destroy Both Soul and Body in Hell' (Matt. 10:28 RSV)." *Expository Times* 81 (1970): 276–82.

McFarland, Bentson H. "Cost-Effectiveness Considerations for Managed Care Systems: Treating Depression in Primary

Care." *American Journal of Medicine* 97 (suppl. 6A) (19 December 1994): 6A–48S.

McLoughlin, William G. *Soul Liberty: The Baptists' Struggle in New England, 1630–1833.* Hanover, N.H.: University Press of New England, 1991.

Mead, Loren B. *Transforming Congregations for the Future.* Washington, D.C.: Alban Institute, 1994.

Medved, Diane. *The Case against Divorce.* New York: Ballantine Books, 1989.

Mendelsohn, I. "Dreams." In *Interpreter's Dictionary of the Bible: An Illustrated Encyclopedia.* 4 vols. plus supplement. Vol. 1, edited by Charles A. Buttrick, Thomas S. Kepler, John Knox, Herbert G. May, Samuel Terrien, and Emory S. Bucke, 868–69. Nashville: Abingdon Press, 1981.

Menninger, Karl. *What Ever Happened to Sin?* New York: Bantam, 1988.

Miller, David, ed. *Jung and the Interpretation of the Bible.* New York: Continuum, 1995.

Minaker, Kenneth L. "The Changing Face of Health Care for the Elderly." Paper presented at the Conference on Geriatric Psychiatry, Harvard Medical School, Boston, September 29, 1995.

Mitchell, Henry H., and Nicholas C. Lewter. *Soul Theology: The Heart of American Black Culture.* Nashville: Abingdon, 1991.

Moody, D. "The Double Face of Death." *Review and Expositor* 58 (1961): 348–66.

Moore, Thomas. *Care of the Soul: A Guide for Cultivating Depth and Sacredness in Everyday Life.* New York: HarperCollins, 1992.

———. *Soul Mates: Honoring the Mysteries of Love and Relationship.* New York: HarperCollins, 1994.

Morgan, T. C. "The Mother of All Muddles: Evangelical Theologians Clash in Public over What Kind of Body Jesus Christ Has Following His Resurrection." *Christianity Today* (5 April 1993): 62–66.

Moynihan, Daniel P. "Defining Deviancy Down." *American Scholar* (winter 1993): 22–24.

Napier, B. D. "Visions." In *Interpreter's Dictionary of the Bible: An Illustrated Encyclopedia*. 4 vols. plus supplement. Vol. 4, edited by Charles A. Buttrick, Thomas S. Kepler, John Knox, Herbert G. May, Samuel Terrien, and Emory S. Bucke, 791. Nashville: Abingdon Press, 1981.

Nee, Watchman. *The Spiritual Man*. New York: Christian Fellowship, 1986.

Niebuhr, Reinhold. *The Nature and Destiny of Man: A Christian Interpretation*. New York: Charles Scribner's Sons, 1949.

Oddenino, Kathy. *A Soul Approach to Depression: Our Normal Transitional Emotions*. Annapolis, Md.: Joy Publications, 1995.

Oken, Alan. *Soul Centered Astrology*. New York: Bantam, 1990.

Oppenheim, A. L. "The Interpretation of Dreams in the Ancient Near East with a Translation of an Assyrian Dream Book." *Transactions of the American Philosophical Society* 46 (1956): 3.

Osei-Bonsu, J. "The Intermediate State in the New Testament." *Scottish Journal of Theology* 44 (1991): 169–94.

"Patients' Spiritual Beliefs Need to Be Recognized in Psychiatric Treatment." *Psychiatric News* (17 March 1995): 9, 22.

Peackock, Heber F. "Translating the Word for 'Soul' in the Old Testament." *Bible Translator* 27 (1976): 216–19.

Pearsall, Susan. "The Rev. Dr. Jeffrey H. Boyd: Psychiatrist and Explorer of the Soul." *New York Times*, 12 March 1995, Connecticut section, CN 3.

Peck, M. Scott. *The Road Less Traveled: A New Psychology of Love, Traditional Values, and Spiritual Growth*. New York: Simon & Schuster, 1988.

Pedersen, Johannes. *Israel: Its Life and Culture*. London: Oxford University Press, 1926.

Penfield, Wilder. *The Mystery of the Mind*. Princeton, N.J.: Princeton University Press, 1975.

Penn-Lewis, Jessie. *Soul and Spirit*. Fort Washington, Pa.: Christian Literature Crusade, 1993.

Phillips, John B. *Your God Is Too Small*. New York: Macmillan, 1964.

Philo. "On the Account of the World's Creation Given by Moses." In *Philo,* 10 vols. Vol. 1, edited by G. P. Goold, translated by F. H. Colson and G. H. Whitaker, 2–139. Cambridge: Harvard University Press, 1991.

Pierpaoli, Walter, William Regelson, and Carol Colman. *The Melatonin Miracle: Nature's Age-Reversing, Disease-Fighting, Sex-Enhancing Hormone.* New York: Simon & Schuster, 1995.

Plato. "Phaedo." In *Plato in Twelve Volumes: Vol. I—Euthyphro, Apology, Crito, Phaedo, Phaedrus,* translated by Harold N. Fowler, 193–404. Cambridge: Harvard University Press, 1982.

———. *Plato: Lysis, Symposium, Gorgias.* Translated by W. R. M. Lamb. Cambridge: Harvard University Press, 1925.

———. *The Republic of Plato.* Translated by Allan Bloom. New York: HarperCollins, 1991.

Plotinus. "Fourth Ennead (On the Soul)." In *Plotinus, the Six Enneads,* vol. 17, translated by Stephen MacKenna and B. S. Page, 139–207. In the series *Great Books of the Western World,* 54 vols. Chicago: William Benton, Encyclopaedia Britannica, 1952.

Popenroe, D. "The Family Condition of America: Cultural Change and Public Policy." In *Values and Public Policy,* edited by H. J. Aaron, T. B. Mann, and T. Taylor, 98–99. Washington, D.C.: Brookings Institution, 1994.

Popper, Karl R., and John C. Eccles. *The Self and Its Brain.* New York: Springer, 1977.

Post, Robert M. "Transduction of Psychosocial Stress into the Neurobiology of Recurrent Affective Disorder." *American Journal of Psychiatry* 149 (1992): 999–1010.

Post, Robert M., and S. R. B. Weiss. "The Neurobiology of Treatment-Resistant Mood Disorders." In *Psychopharmacology: The Fourth Generation of Progress,* edited by F. E. Bloom and D. J. Kupfer, 1155–70. New York: Raven Press, 1995.

Propst, L. Rebecca, Richard Ostrom, Philip Watkins, Terri Dean, and David Mashburn. "Comparative Efficacy of Religious and Nonreligious Cognitive-Behavioral Therapy for the Treatment of Clinical Depression in Religious Individuals." *Journal of Consulting and Clinical Psychology* 60 (1992): 94–103.

Purdy, Alexander C. "Paul the Apostle." In *Interpreter's Dictionary of the Bible: An Illustrated Encyclopedia*. 4 vols. plus supplement. Vol. 3, edited by Charles A. Buttrick, Thomas S. Kepler, John Knox, Herbert G. May, Samuel Terrien, and Emory S. Bucke, 681–704. Nashville: Abingdon Press, 1981.

Ragan, Claude, H. Newton Malony, and Benjamin Bert-Hallahmi. "Psychologists and Religion: Professional Factors and Personal Belief." *Review of Religious Research* 21 (spring 1980): 208–17.

Rahner, Karl. *On the Meaning of Death*. New York: Herder & Herder, 1961.

Raphael, Simcha Paull. "Is There Afterlife after Auschwitz? Reflections on Life after Death in the 20th Century." *Judaism* 44 (1992): 346–60.

Raspberry, William. "Out of Wedlock, Out of Luck." *Washington Post*, 25 February 1994, A21.

Reed, Ralph. *Politically Incorrect: The Emerging Faith Factor in American Politics*. Dallas: Word Publishing, 1994.

Rieff, Philip. *The Triumph of the Therapeutic: Uses of Faith After Freud*. Chicago: University of Chicago Press, 1987.

Robinson, J. A. T. *The Body: A Study in Pauline Theology*. Chicago: Regnery, 1952.

Rollins, Wayne G. *Jung and the Bible*. Louisville: Westminster John Knox, 1983.

Rosenthal, N. "Molecular Medicine: Regulation of Gene Expression." *New England Journal of Medicine* 331 (6 October 1994): 931–33.

Sachs, Jacqueline S. "Recognition Memory for Syntactic and Semantic Aspects of Connected Discourse." *Perception and Psychophysics* 2 (February 1967): 437–42.

Sanford, John A. *Soul Journey: A Jungian Analyst Looks at Reincarnation*. New York: Crossroad, 1991.

Schiedermayer, David. *Putting the Soul Back in Medicine: Reflections on Compassion and Ethics*. Grand Rapids, Mich.: Baker Books, 1994.

Schuller, Robert H. *Self-Esteem: The New Reformation*. Waco, Tex.: Word Books, 1982.

Schwartz, Pepper. "Parent and Child: When Staying Is Worth the Pain." *New York Times*, Connecticut section, 20 April 1995, C1, C4.

Schweizer, Eduard. "New Testament Usage [of *Psyche*] in Distinction from *Pneuma*." In *Theological Dictionary of the New Testament*, vol. 9, edited by Gerhard Friedrich, translated by Geoffrey W. Bromiley, 654–55. Grand Rapids, Mich.: Eerdmans, 1974.

Segal, R. A., ed. *Jung: Gnostic*. Princeton, N.J.: Princeton University Press, 1992.

Sellner, Edward. *Soul-Making: The Telling of a Spiritual Journey*. Mystic, Conn.: Twenty-Third Publishers, 1991.

Sheed, Frank J. *Theology for Beginners*. Ann Arbor: Servant, 1982.

Shengold, Leonard. *Soul Murder: Effects of Childhood Abuse and Deprivation*. New York: Fawcett, 1991.

Shewmon, D. A. "The Metaphysics of Brain Death, Persistent Vegetative State and Dementia." *Thomist* 49 (1985): 24–80.

Smith, Ph. "Brain Death: A Thomistic Appraisal." *Angelicum* 67 (1990): 3–36.

Smith, Rosamond. *Soul-Mate*. New York: NAL-Dutton, 1990.

Sproul, R. C. *Soul's Quest for God*. Wheaton, Ill.: Tyndale, 1993.

Stein, Murray. "The Gnostic Critique, Past and Present." In *The Allure of Gnosticism*, edited by R. A. Segal, J. Singer, and Murray Stein. Chicago: Open Court, 1995.

———. *Jung's Treatment of Christianity: The Psychotherapy of a Religious Tradition*. Wilmette, Ill.: Chiron, 1985.

Stendahl, Krister. *Energy for Life*. Geneva: WCC Publications, 1990.

———. "Immortality Is Too Much and Too Little." In *Meanings: The Bible as Document and Guide*, 193–202. Minneapolis: Augsburg Fortress Press, 1984

———. *The School of Saint Matthew*. Ramsey, N.J.: Sigler Press, 1991.

———, ed. *Immortality and Resurrection.* New York: Macmillan, 1965.

Tertullian. *De Anima.* Edited by J. H. Waszink. Amsterdam: J. M. Meulenhoff, 1947.

Theological Commission. "Some Current Questions in Eschatology." *Irish Theological Quarterly* 58 (1992): 209–43.

Thomsen, Robert. *Bill W.* New York: Harper & Row, 1985.

Tilby, Angela. *Soul: God, Self, and the New Cosmology.* New York: Doubleday, 1993.

Torrey, E. Fuller. *Freudian Fraud: The Malignant Effect of Freud's Theory on American Thought and Culture.* New York: HarperCollins, 1992.

Van Leeuwen, Mary S. *The Person in Psychology: A Contemporary Christian Appraisal.* Grand Rapids, Mich.: Eerdmans, 1985.

Vitz, Paul C. *Psychology as Religion: The Cult of Self Worship.* Grand Rapids, Mich.: Eerdmans, 1994.

Wallerstein, Judith S. "Children after Divorce: Wounds That Don't Heal." *New York Times Magazine,* 22 January 1989, 18–21, 41–44.

Wasylenki, D. A. "The Cost of Schizophrenia." *Canadian Journal of Psychiatry* 39 (9 Suppl. 2) (November 1994): S65–69.

Weatherhead, Leslie D. *The Will of God.* Nashville: Abingdon Press, 1976.

Weathers, R. S. "Dualism or Holism? A Look at Biblical Anthropology, Ethics, and Human Health." *Journal of the American Scientific Affiliation* 35 (1983): 80–83.

Wells, David F. *No Place for Truth: Or Whatever Happened to Evangelical Theology?* Grand Rapids, Mich.: Eerdmans, 1993.

White, Ernest. *Christian Life and the Unconscious.* New York: Harper & Brothers, 1955.

White, H. V. "Immortality and Resurrection in Recent Theology." *Encounter* 22 (1961): 52–58.

Whitehead, Barbara D. "Dan Quayle Was Right." *The Atlantic,* April 1993, 47–84.

Wiesel, Elie. *Souls on Fire: Portraits and Legends of Hasidic Masters.* Northvale, N.J.: Aronson, 1993.

Winkler, Gershon. *Soul of the Matter: A Jewish-Kabbalistic Perspective on the Human Soul Before, During, and After "Life."* Brooklyn, N.Y.: Judaica Press, 1992.

Wolf, Ernest S. *Treating the Self: Elements of Clinical Self Psychology.* New York: Guilford Press, 1988.

Wolff, Hans Walter. *Anthropology of the Old Testament.* Philadelphia: Fortress Press, 1974.

Woznicki, A. *A Christian Humanism: Karol Wojtyla's Existential Personalism.* New Britain, Conn.: Mariel, 1980.

Yoffe, Emily. "How the Soul Is Sold: James Hillman Developed a Psychoanalytic Theory Few Could Understand, Until His Protégé Thomas Moore Translated It for the Masses." *New York Times Magazine,* 23 April 1995, 44–49.

Zorn, R. O. "II Corinthians 5:1–10: Individual Eschatology or Corporate Solidarity, Which?" *Reformed Theological Review* 48 (1989): 93–104.

INDEX